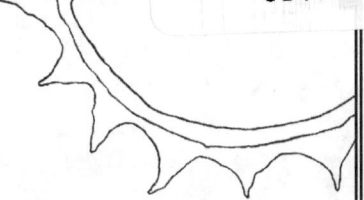

Chickens!

Illustrated Chicken Breeds

A to Z

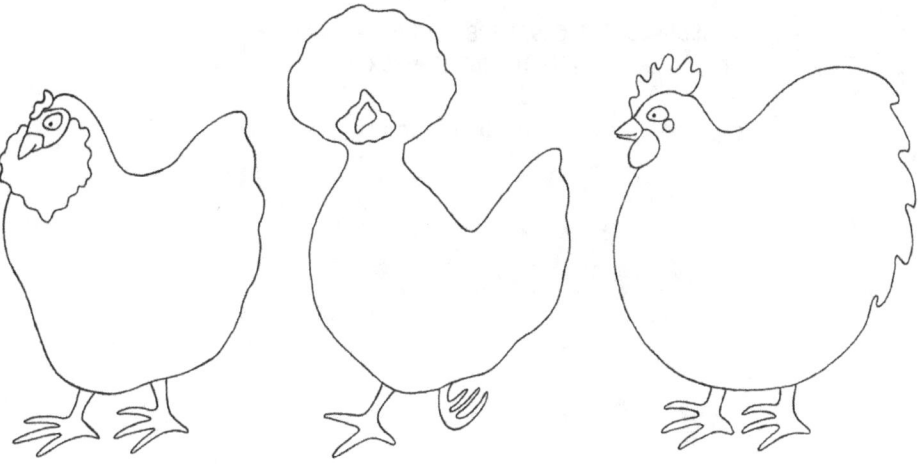

COLORING BOOK

Written and Illustrated by Sarah Rosedahl

ISBN-13: 978-0692559857 (Tolba Farm Press)
ISBN-10: 069255985X

www.srosedahl.com

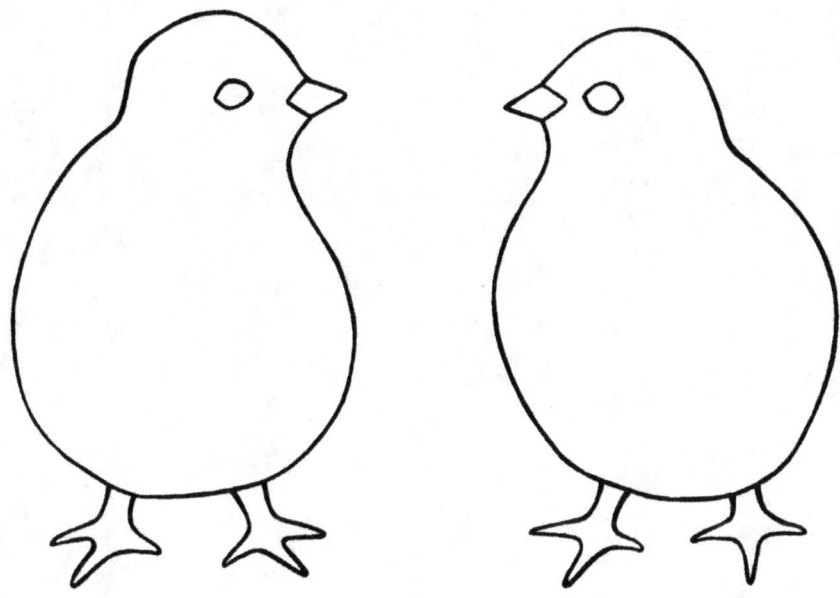

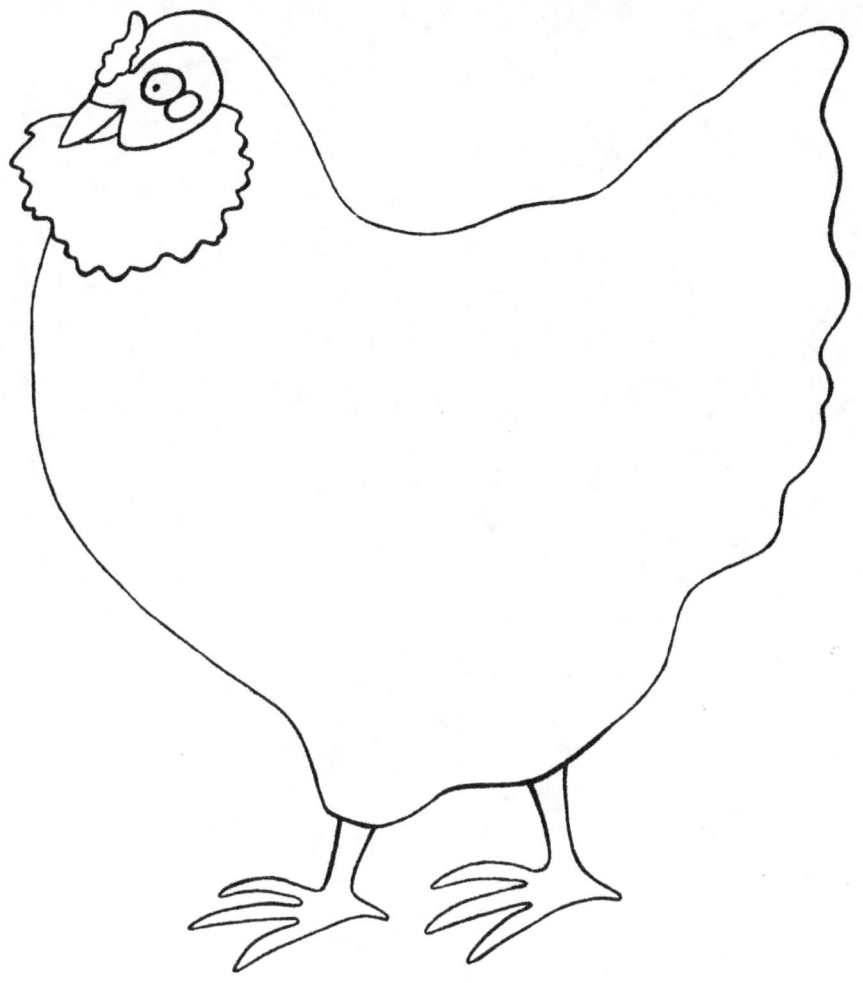

Ameraucana

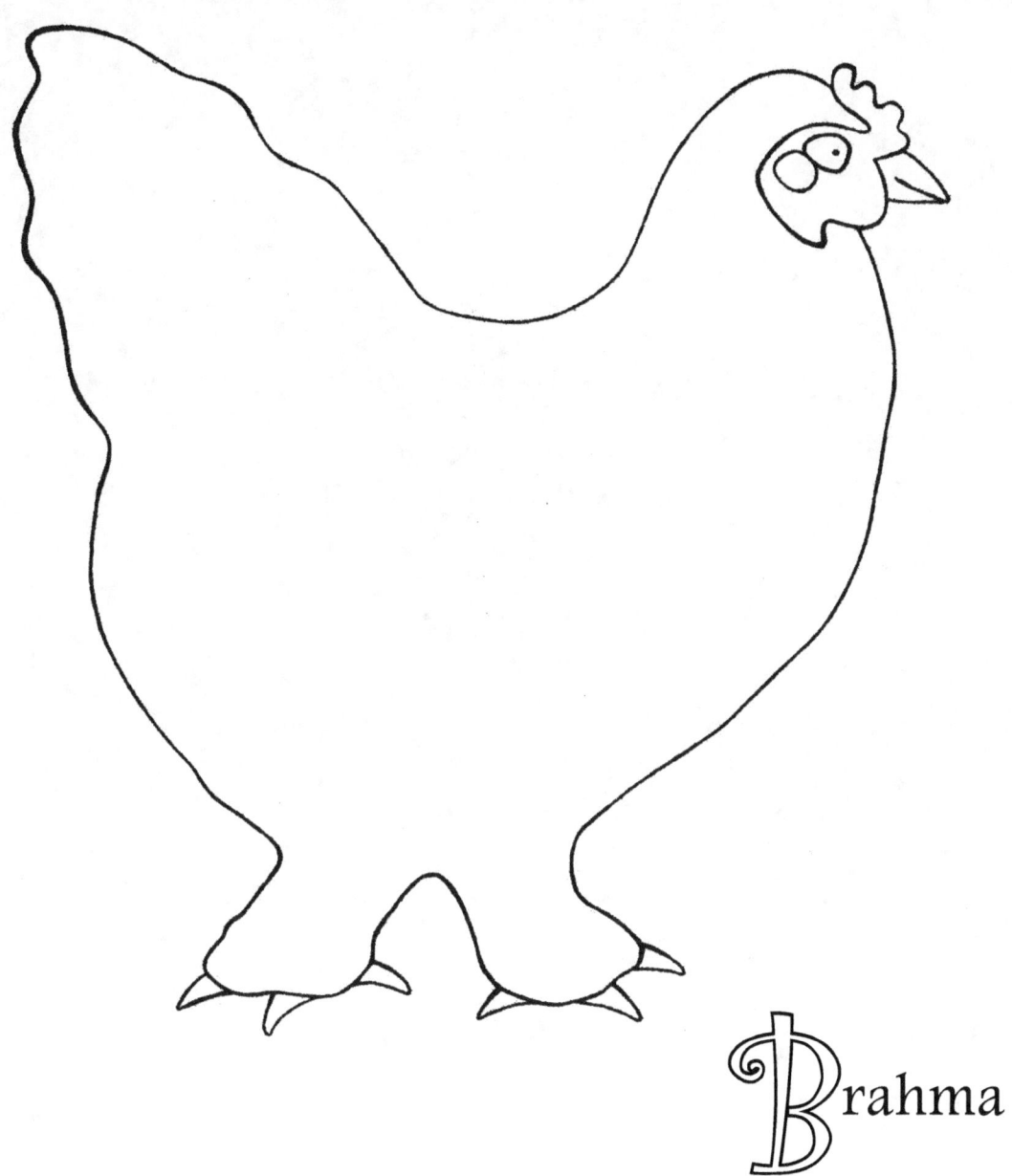

Brahma

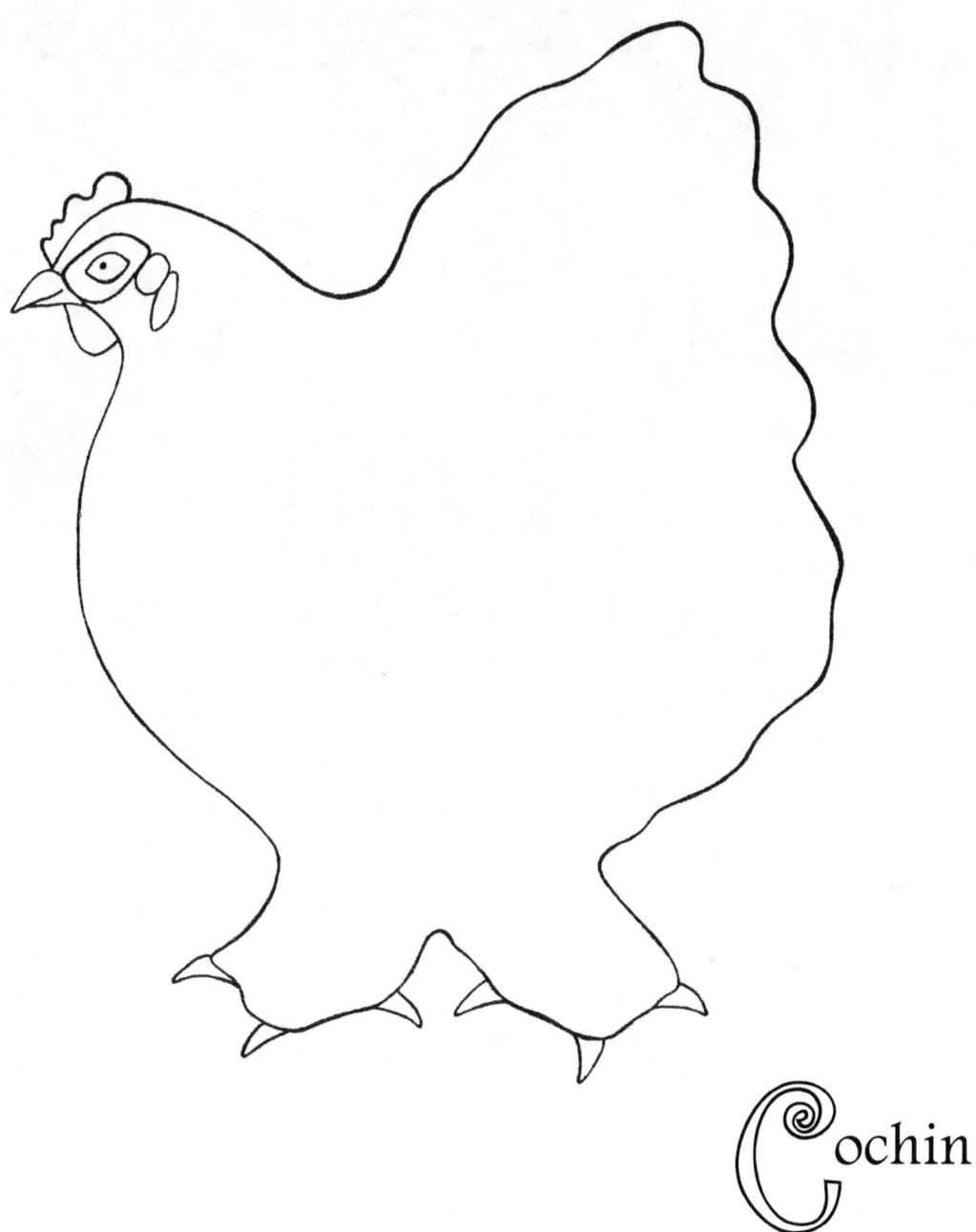

Cochin

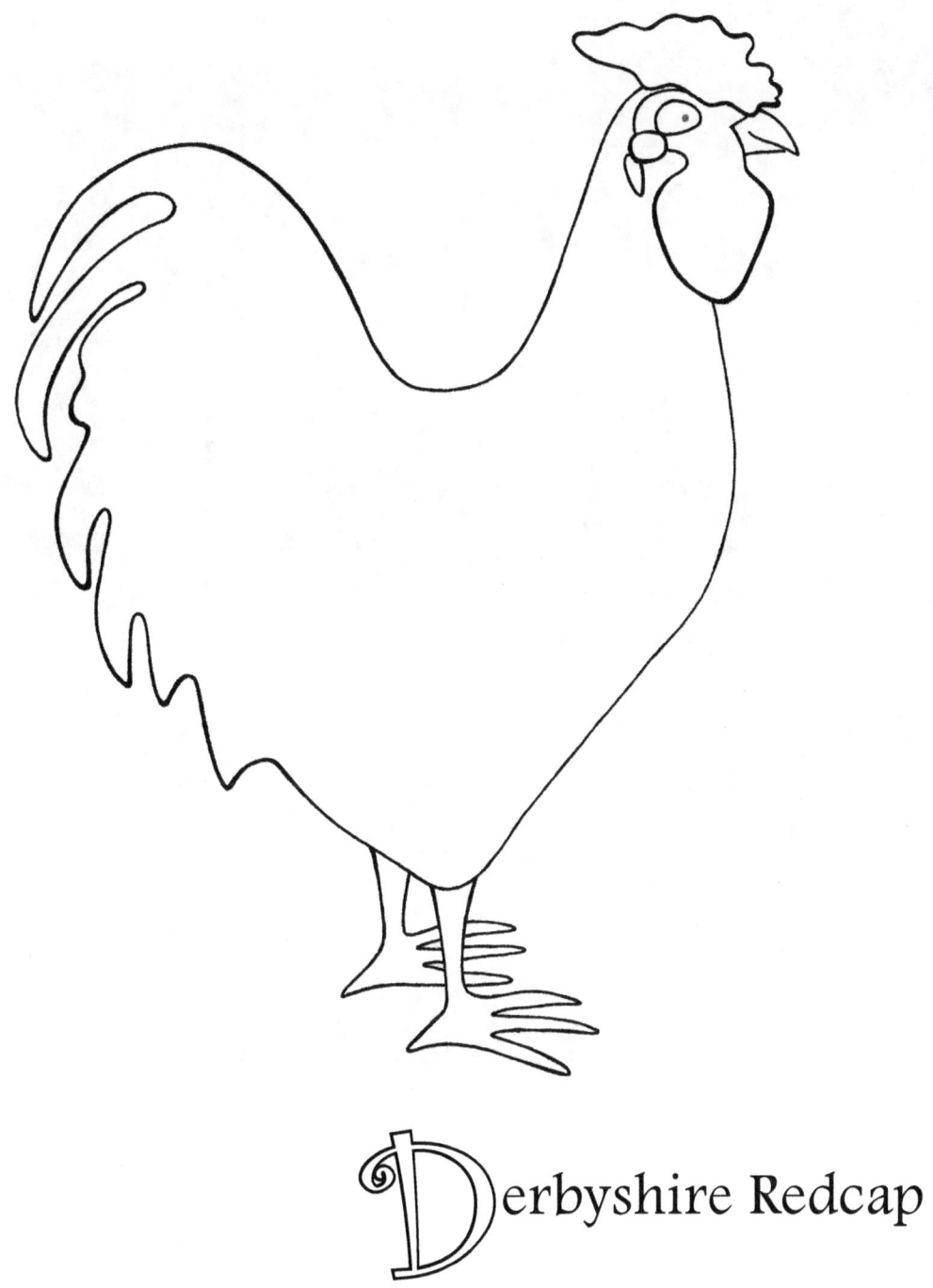

Derbyshire Redcap

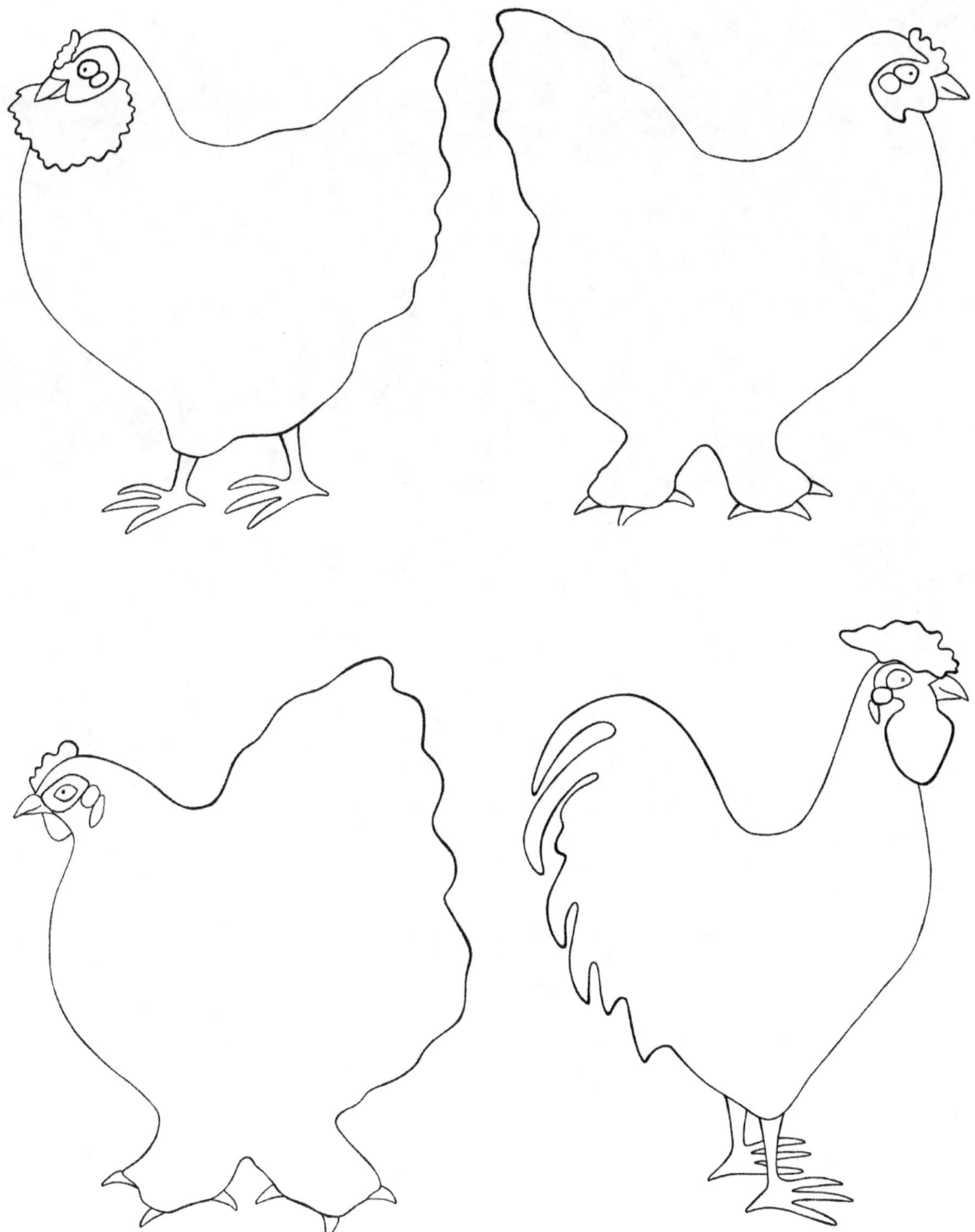

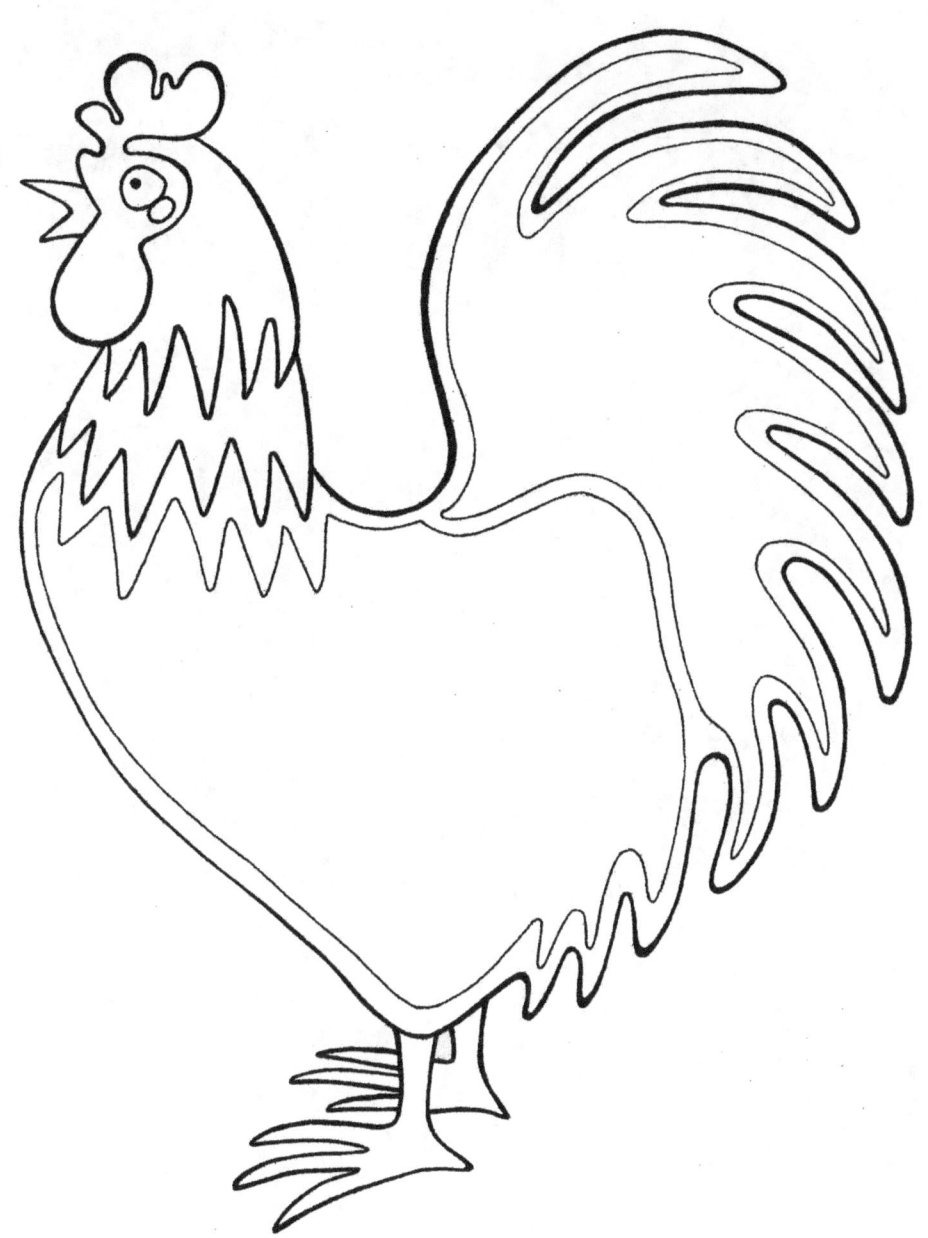

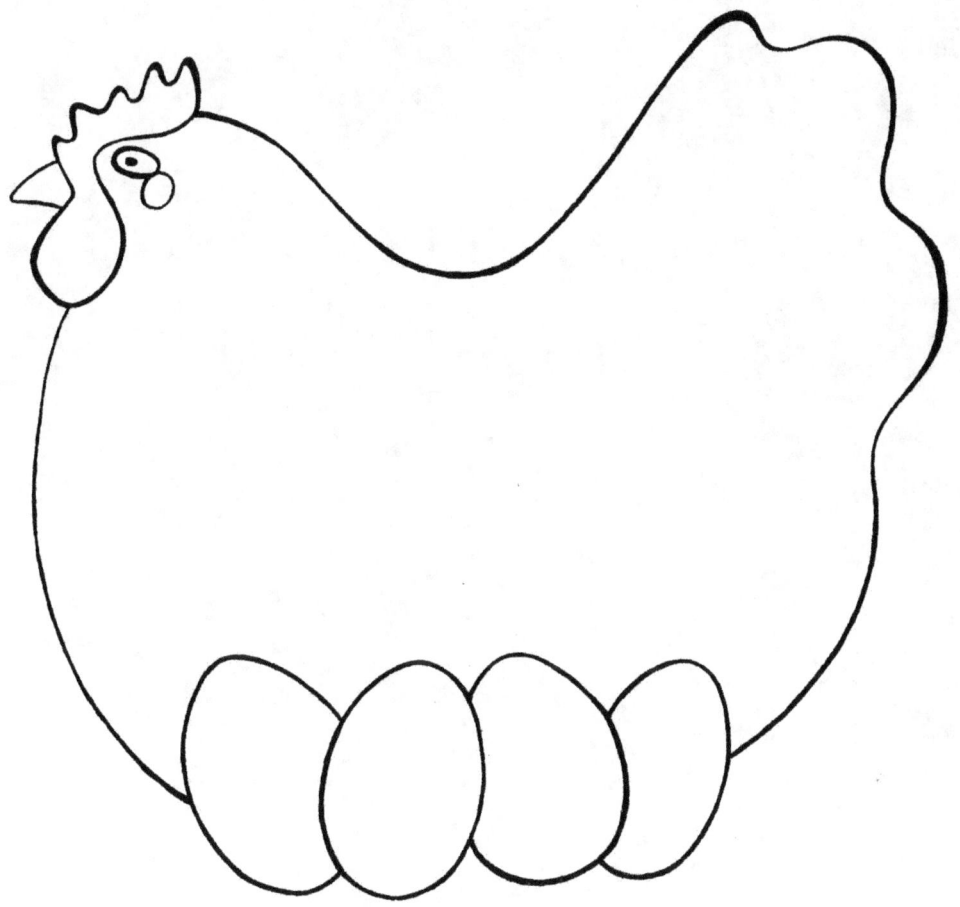

Easter Egger

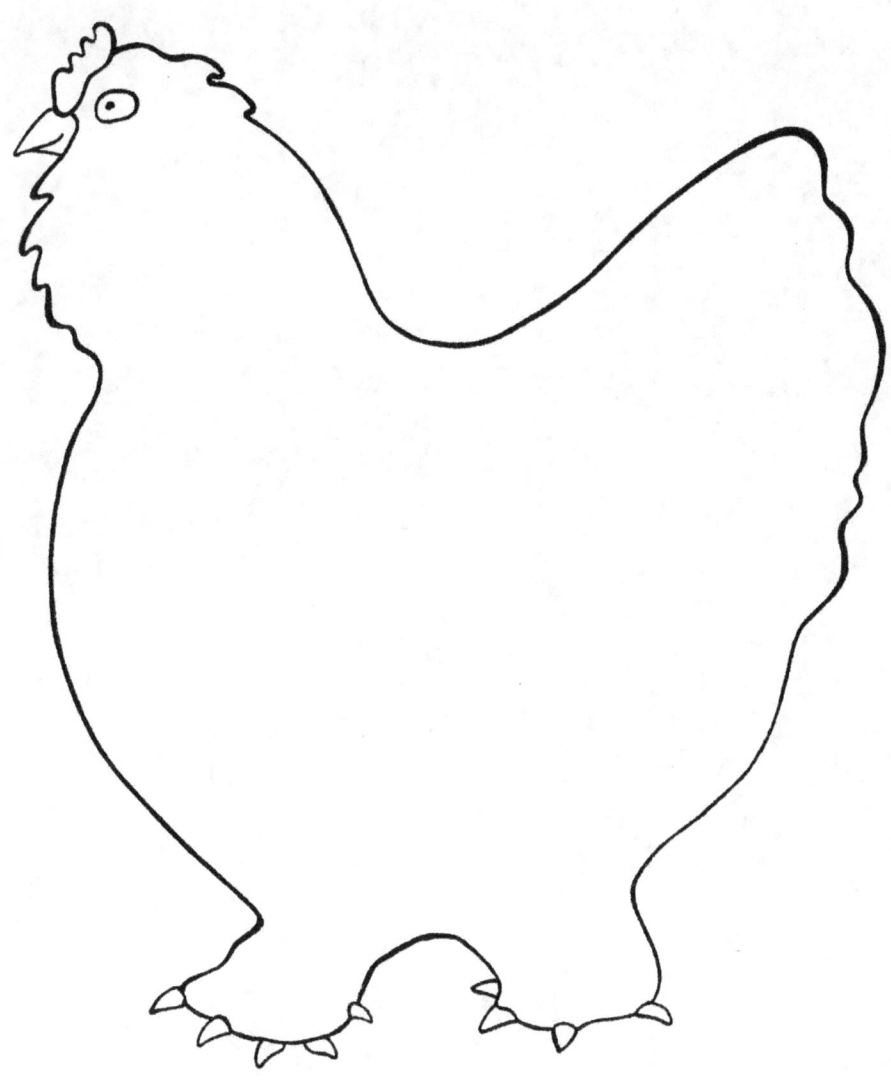

Faverolles

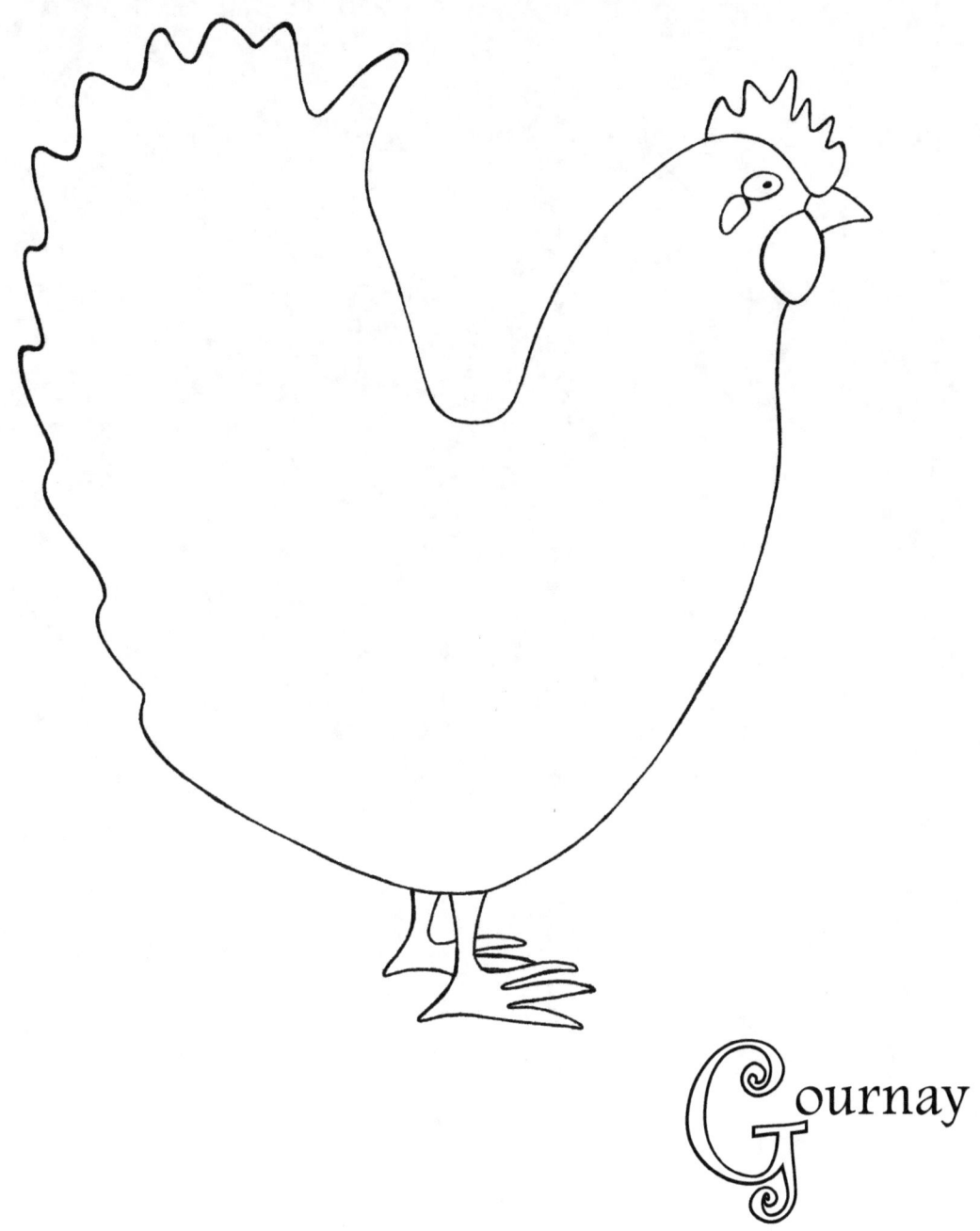

Gournay

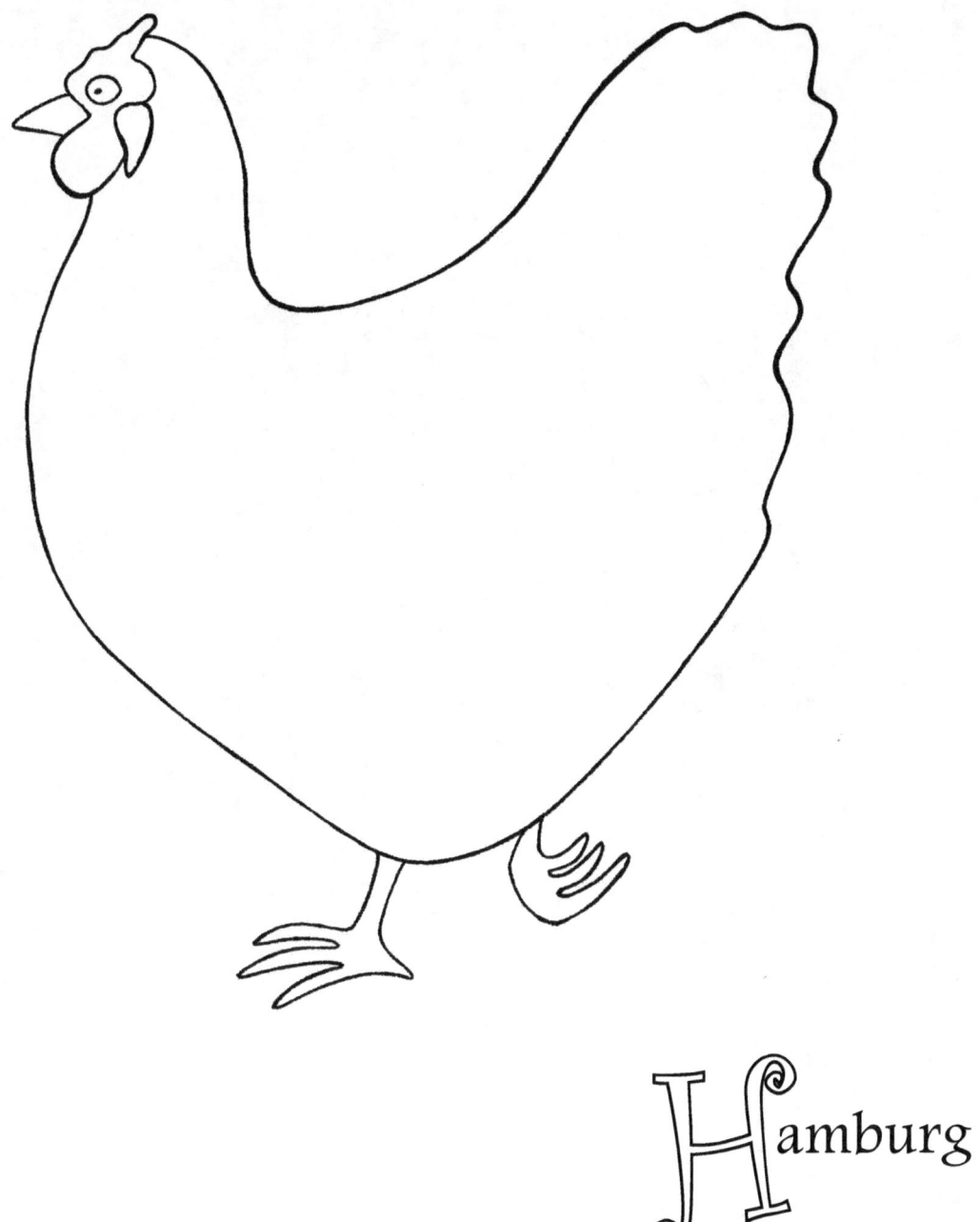

Hamburg

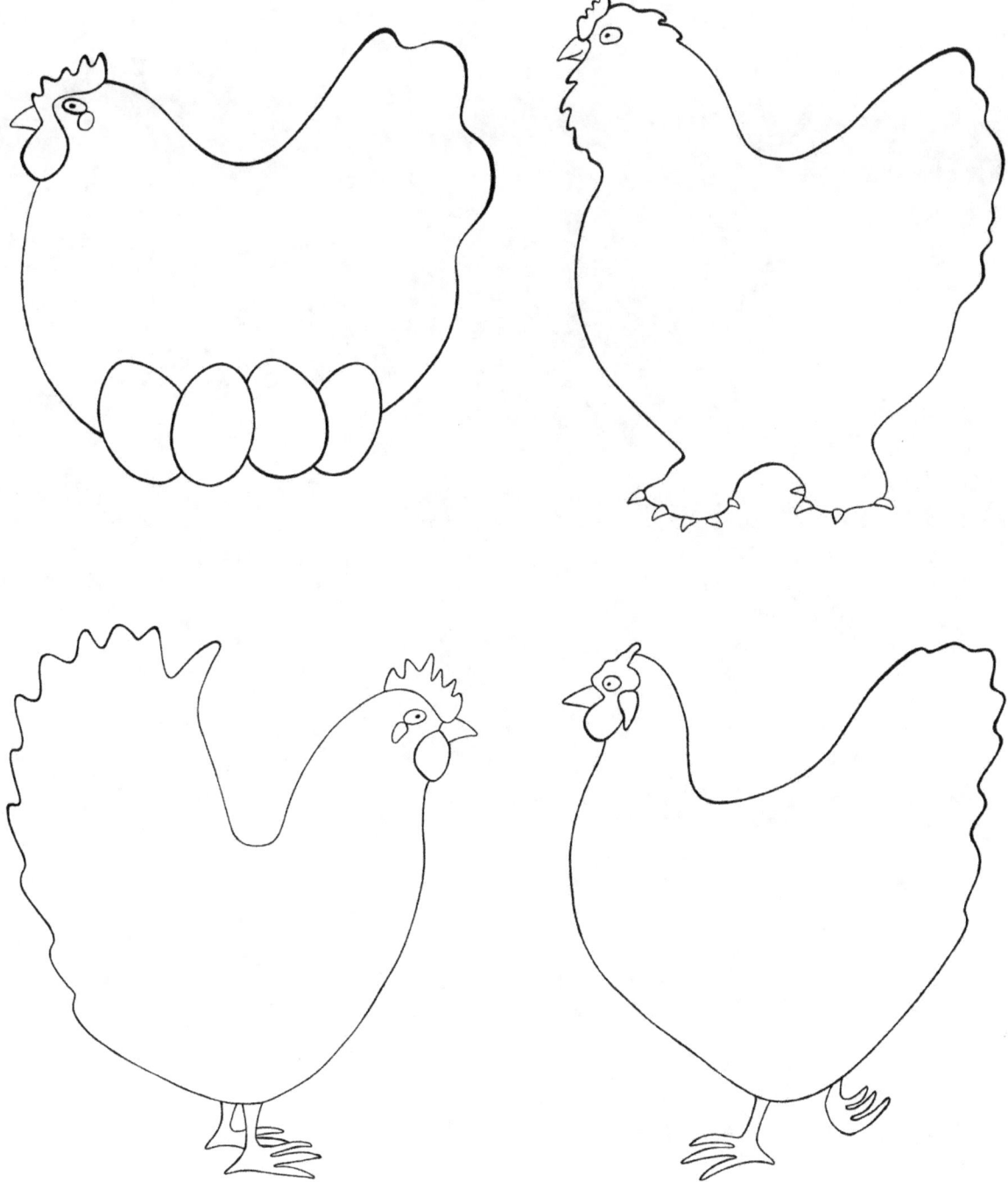

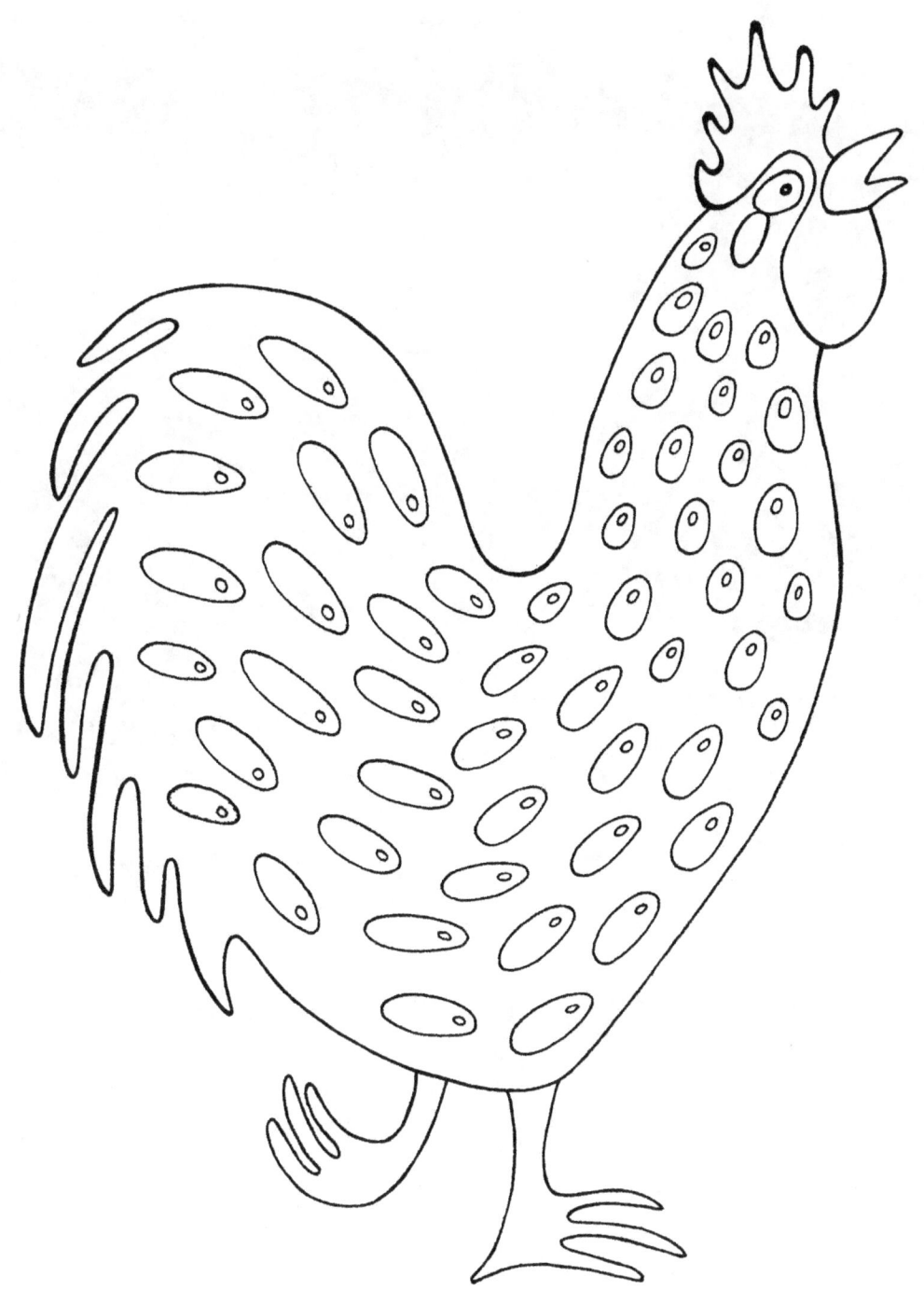

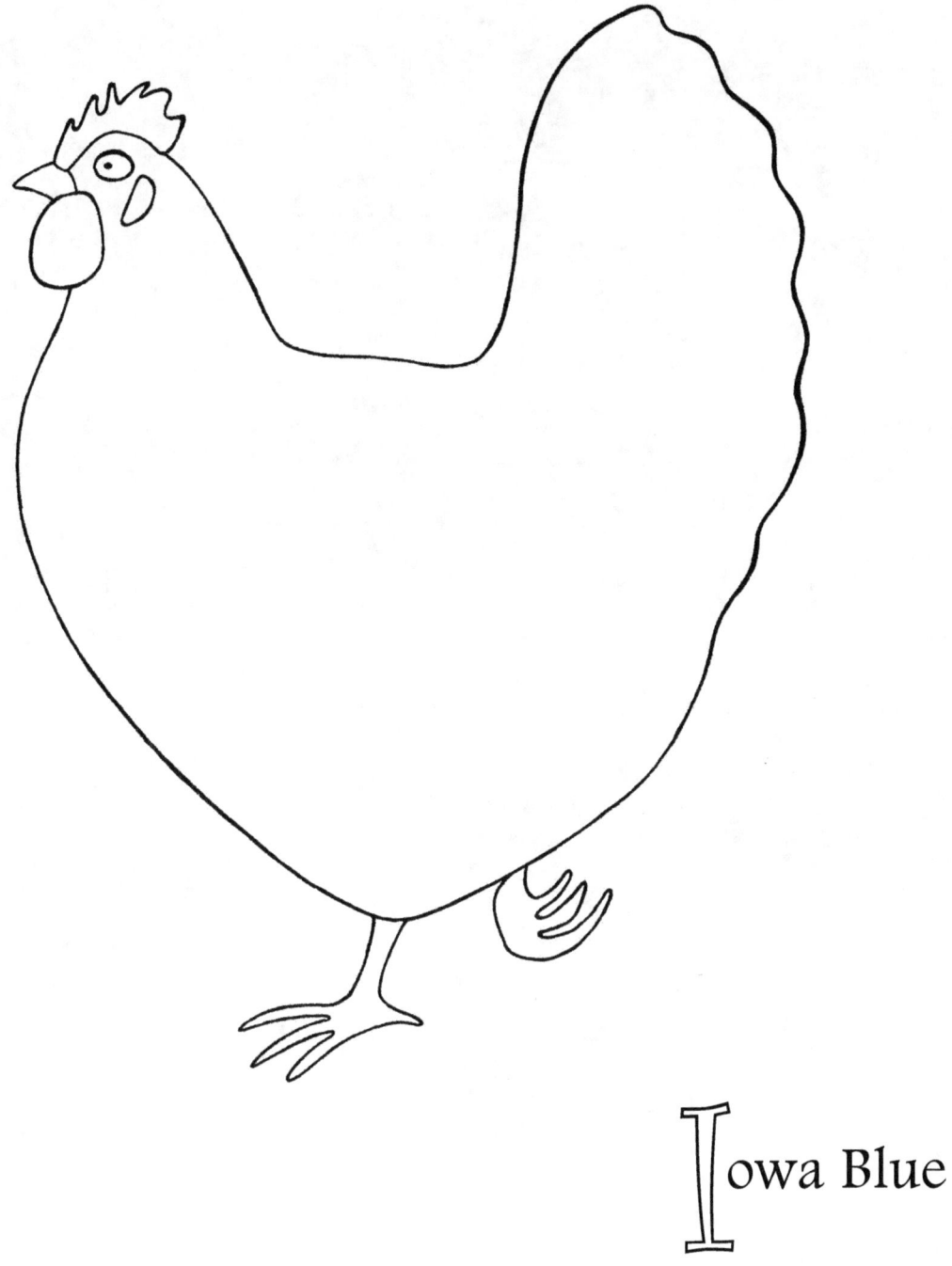

Iowa Blue

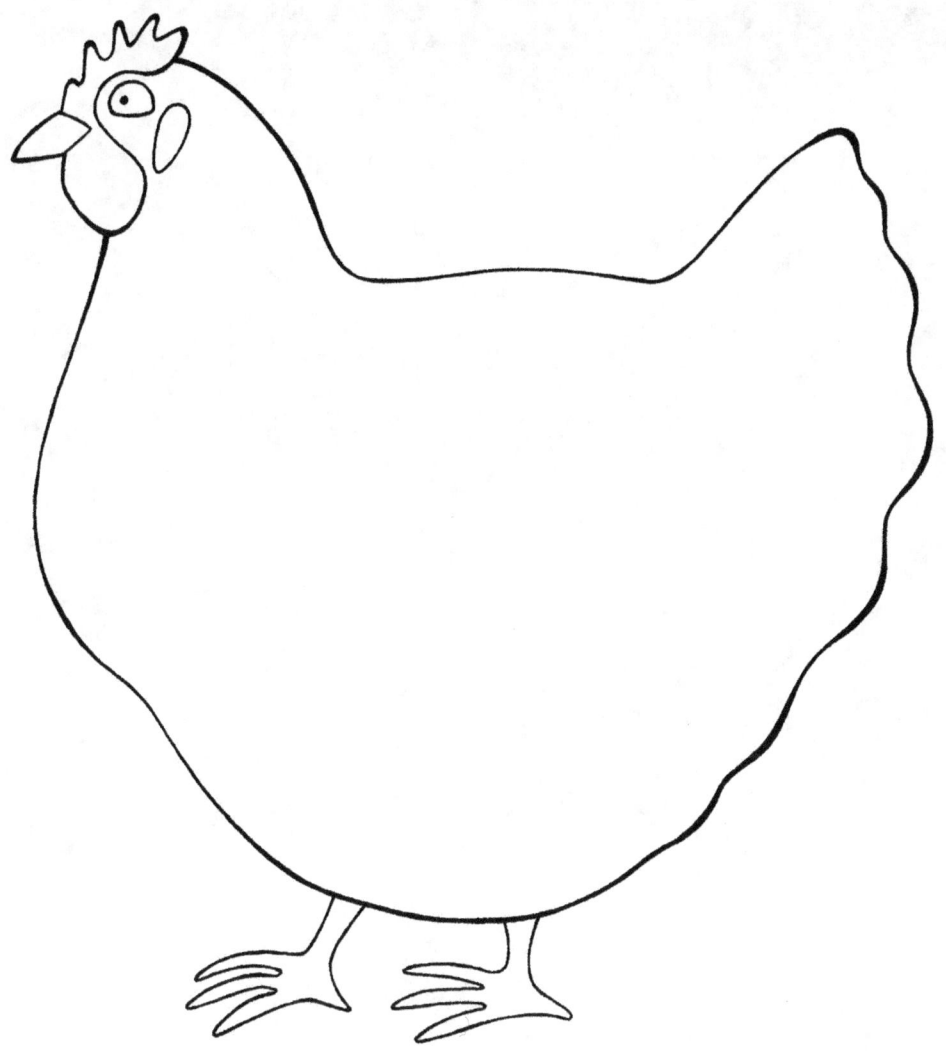

Jersey Giant

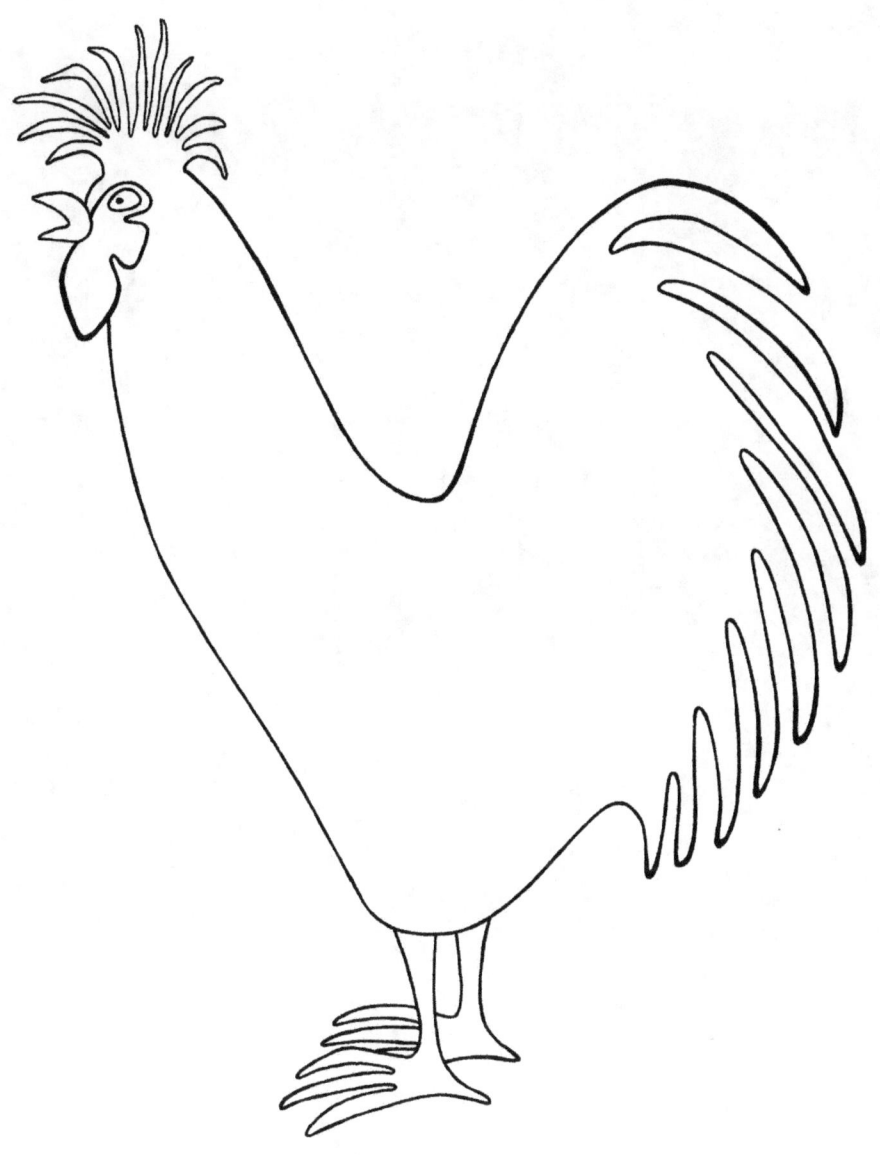

Kosovo Long Crowing Rooster

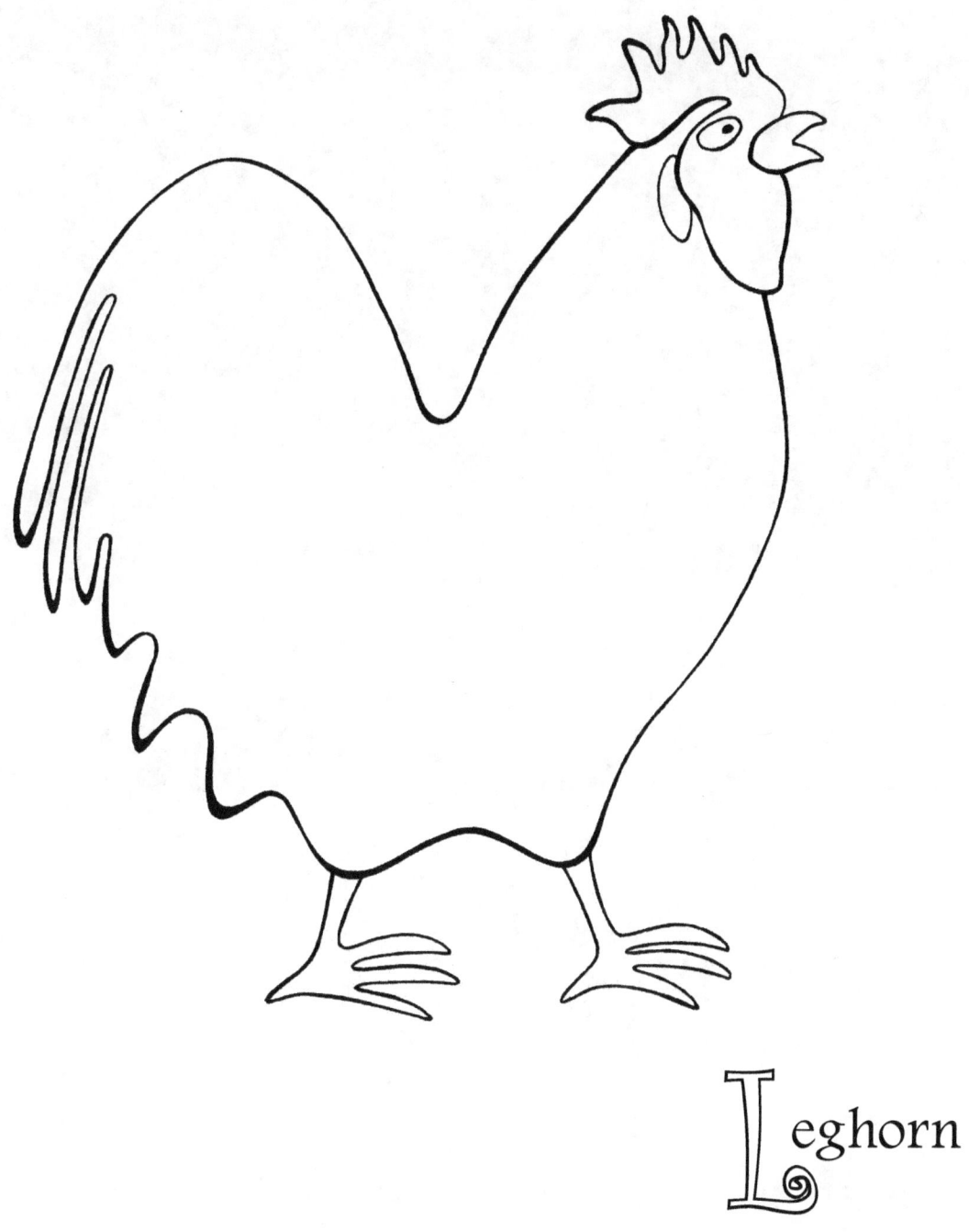

Leghorn

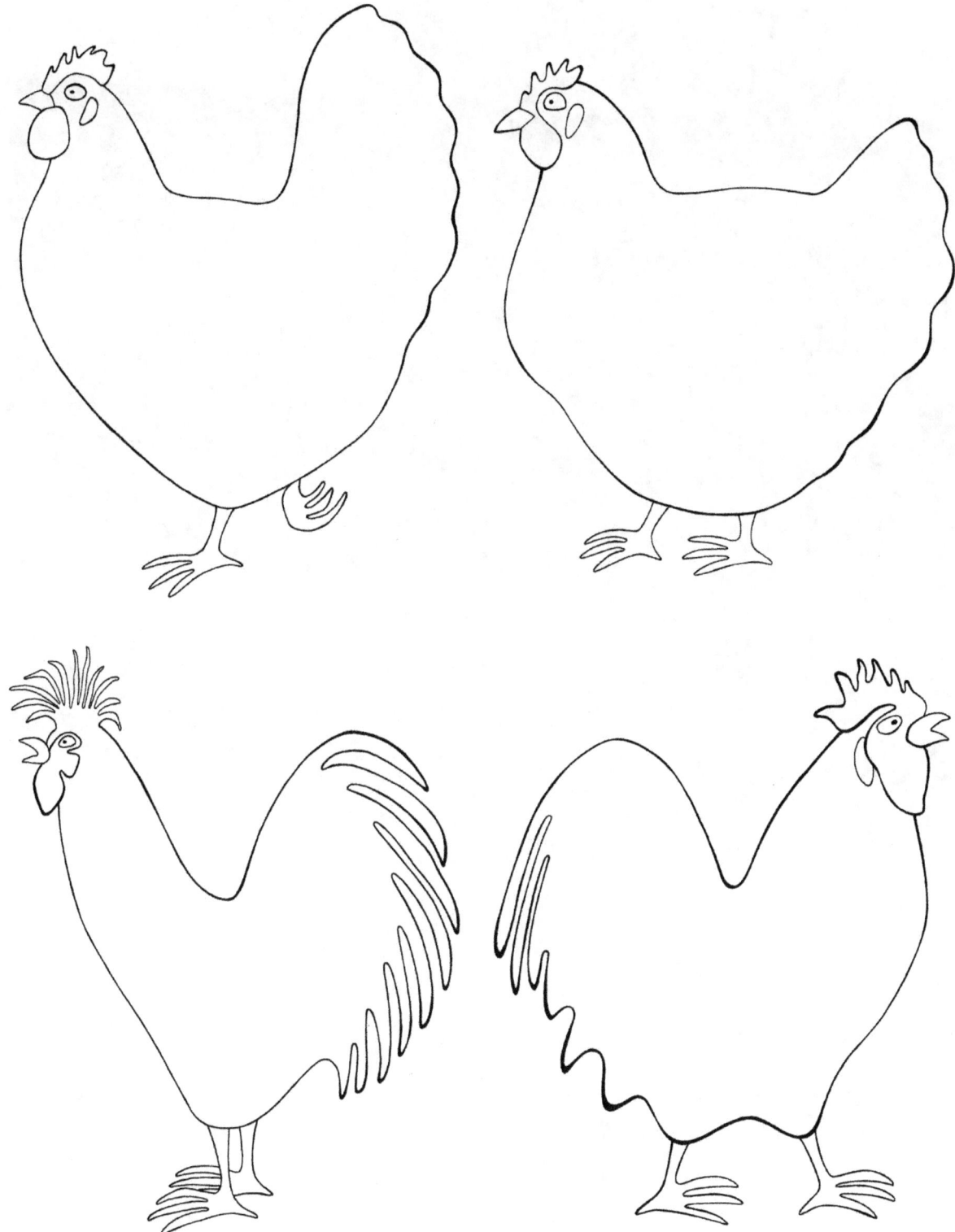

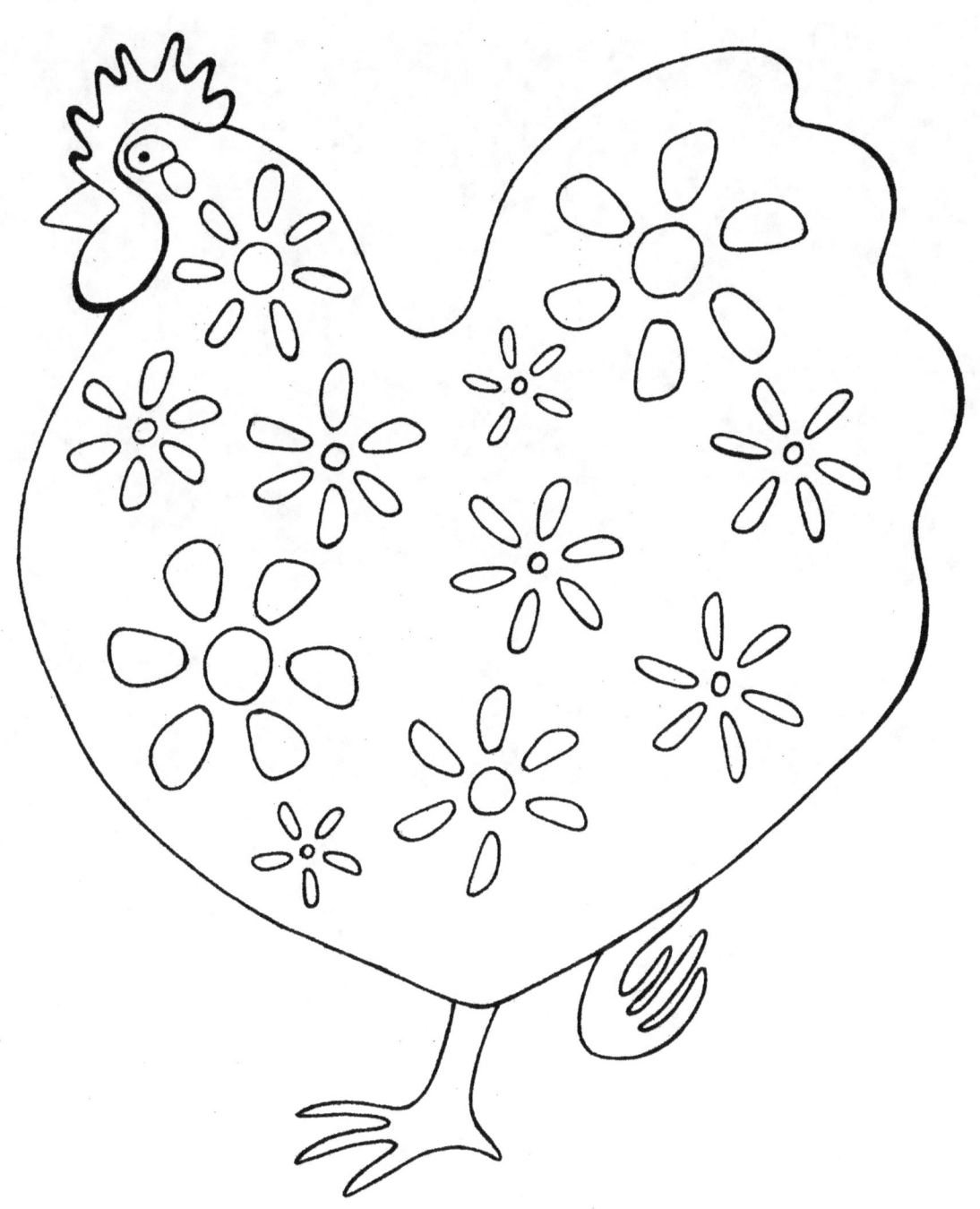

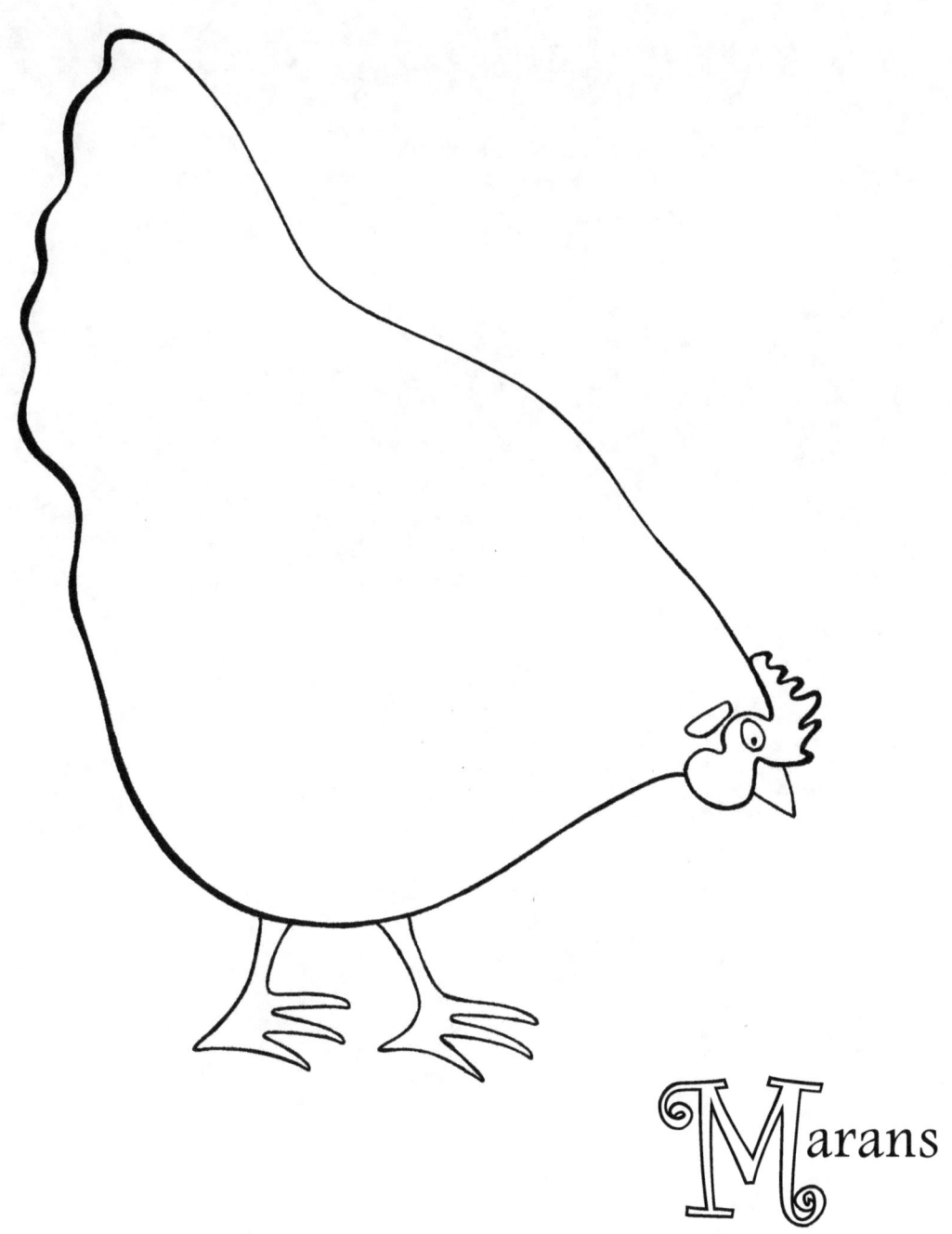

Marans

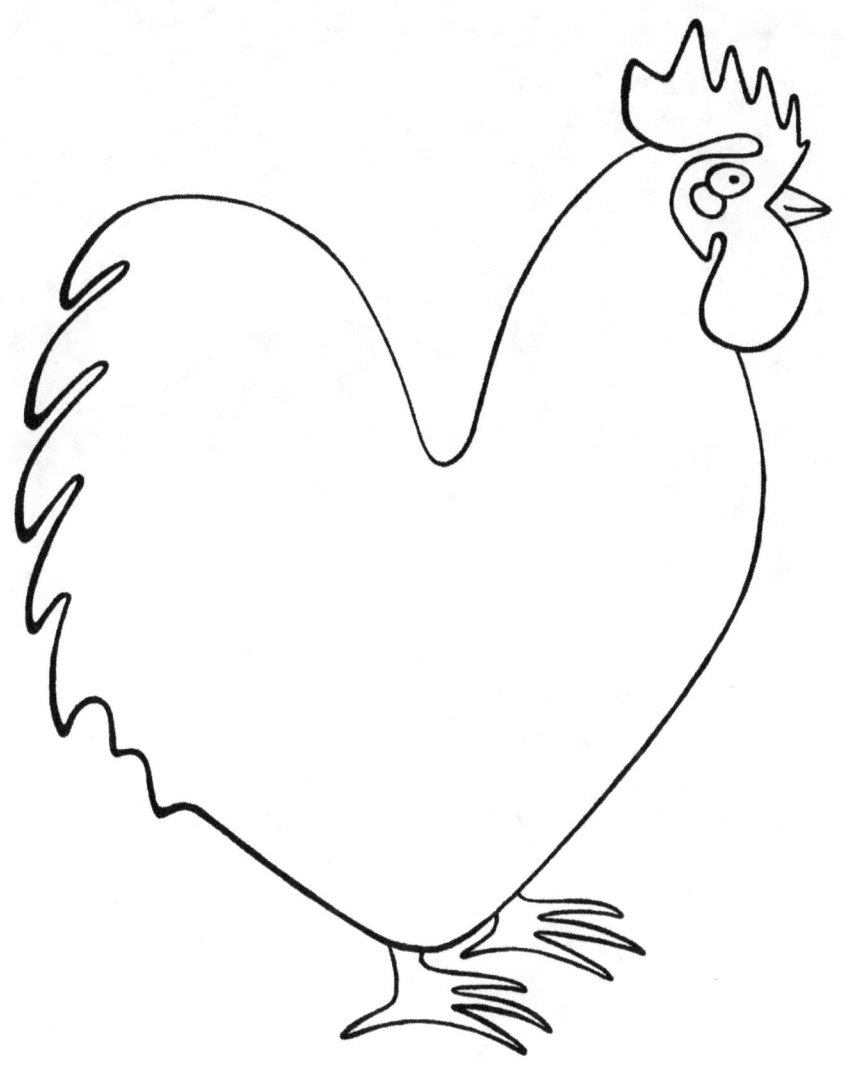

New Hampshire Red

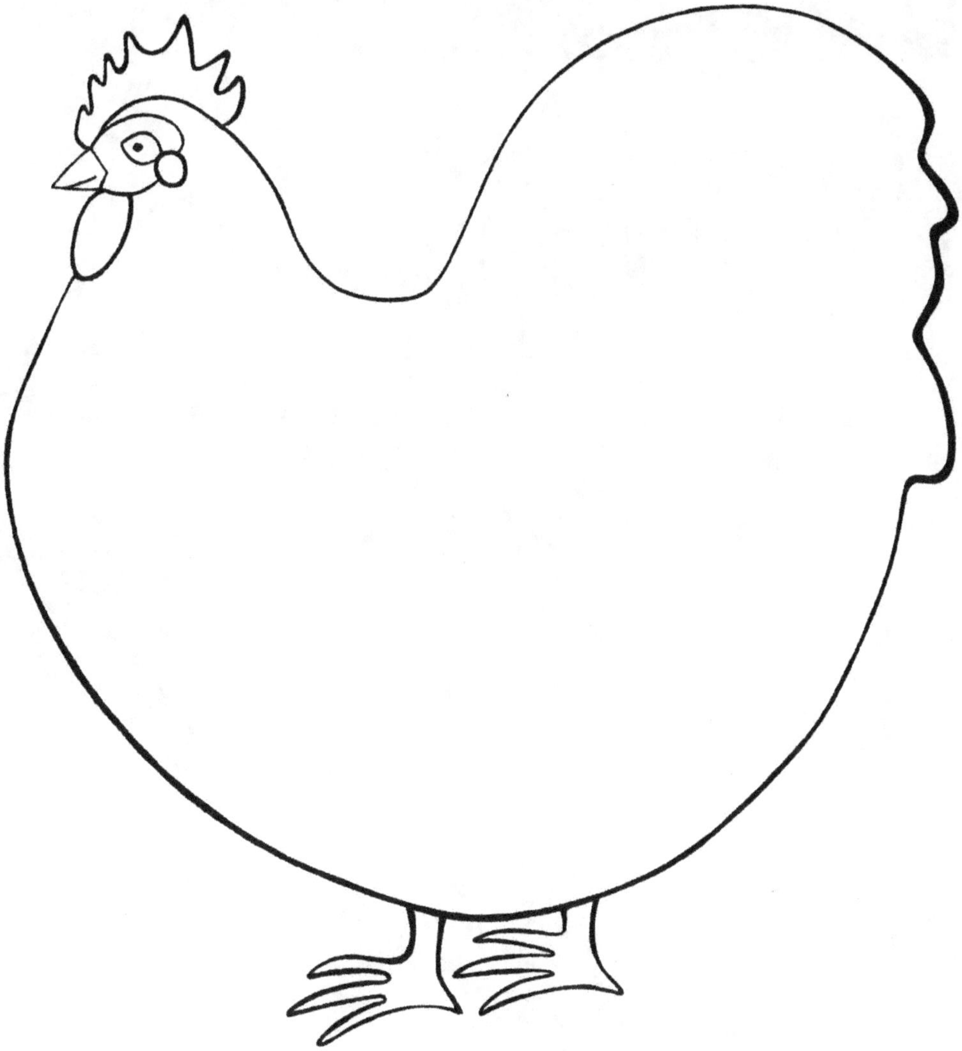

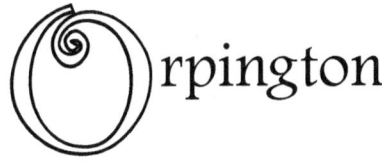
Orpington

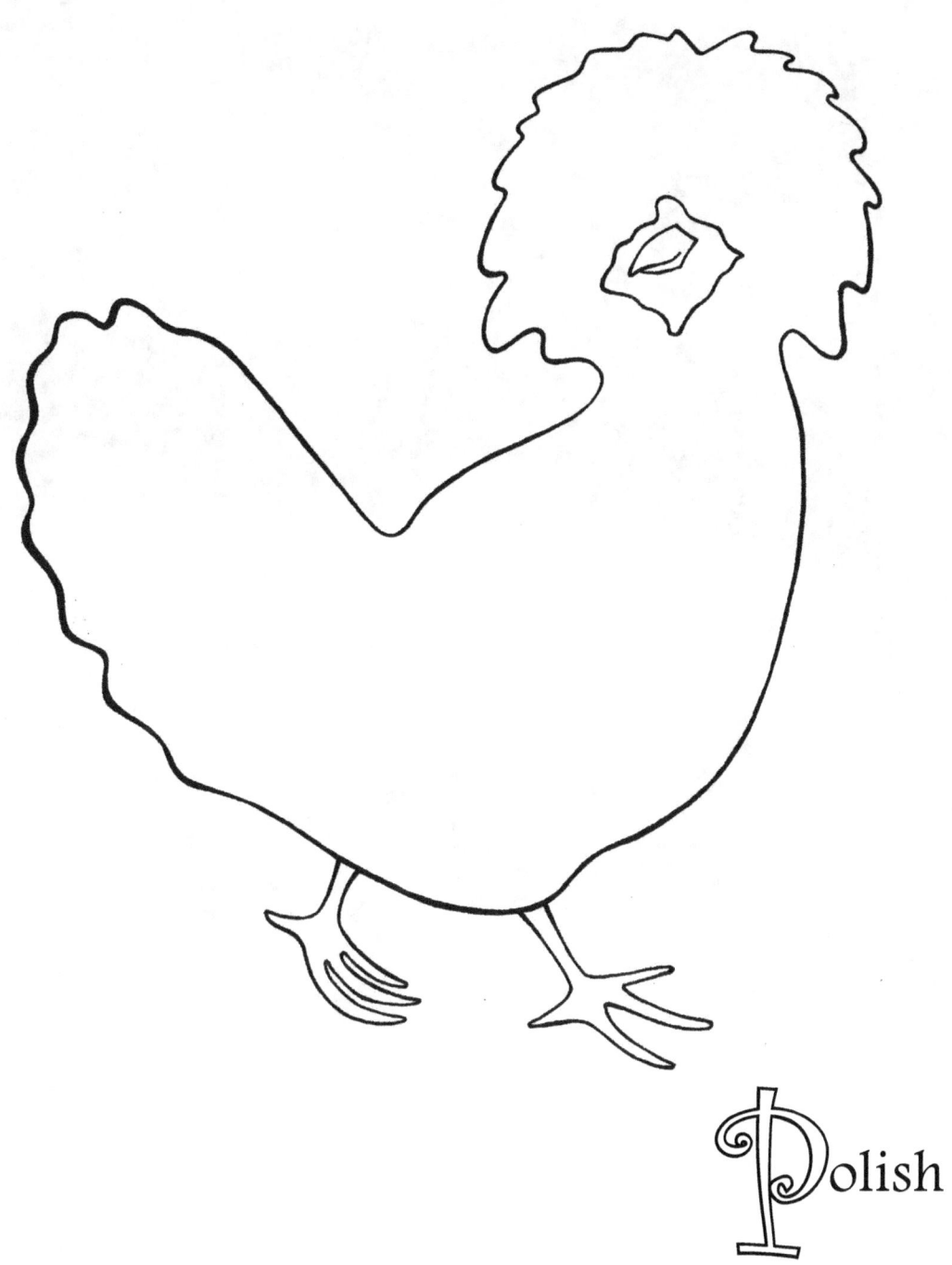

Polish

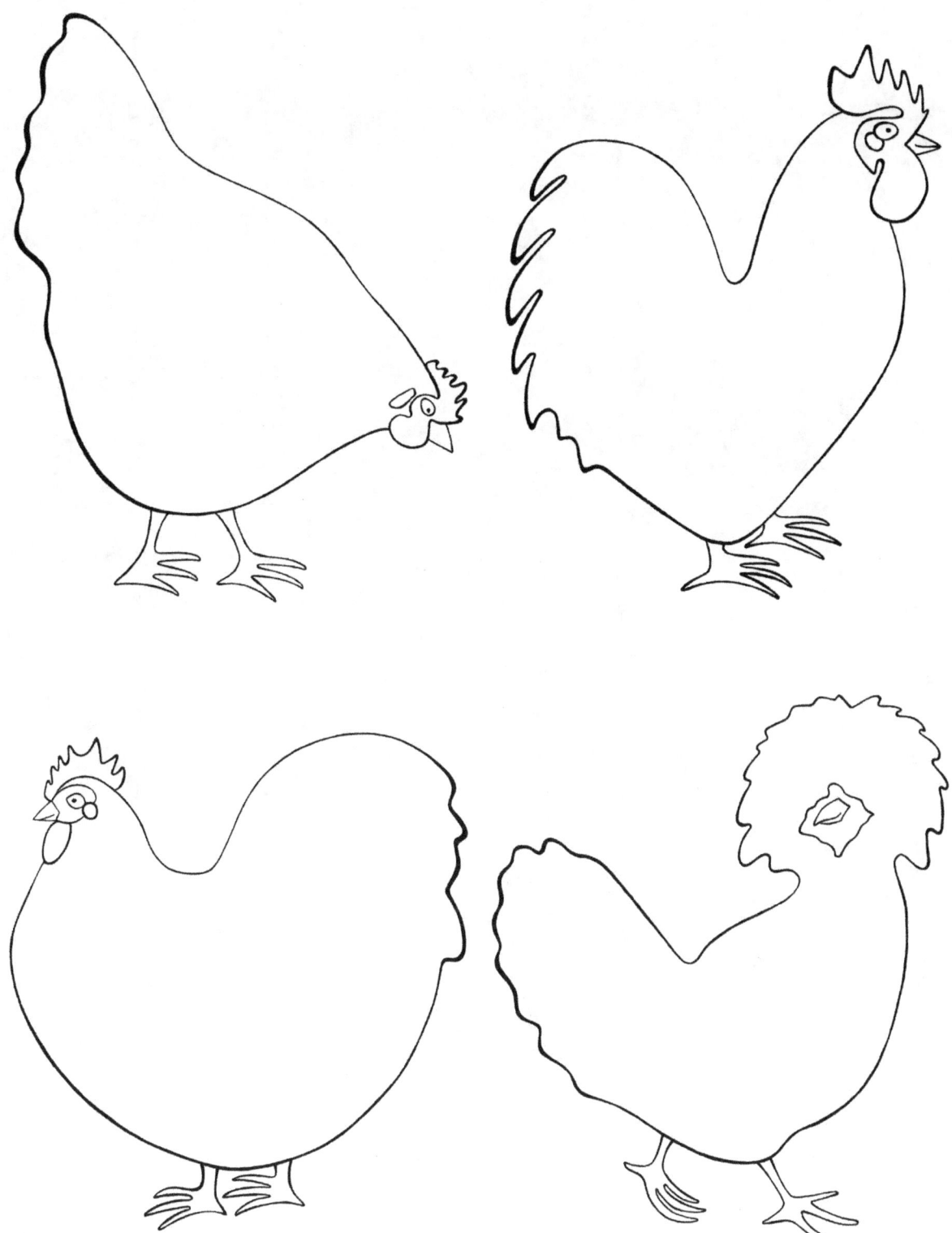

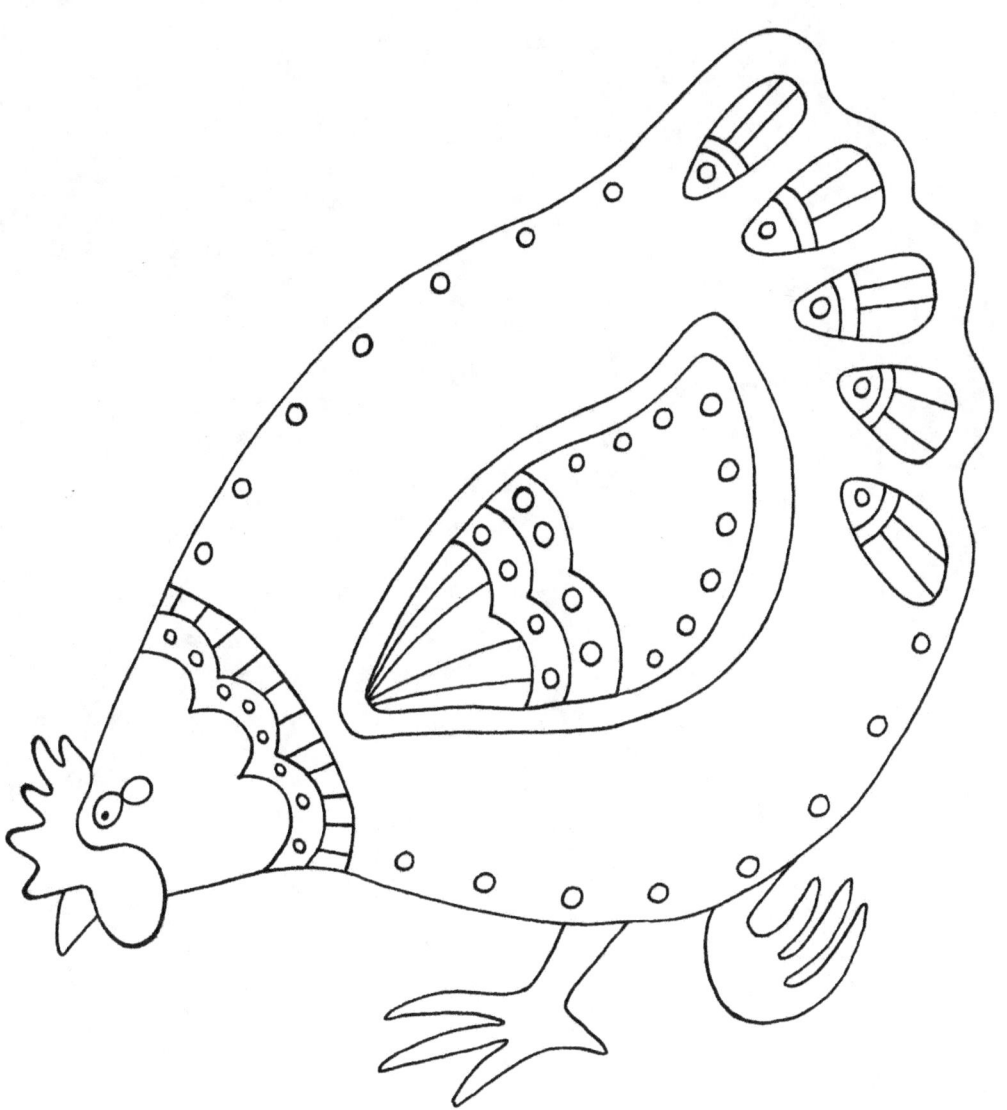

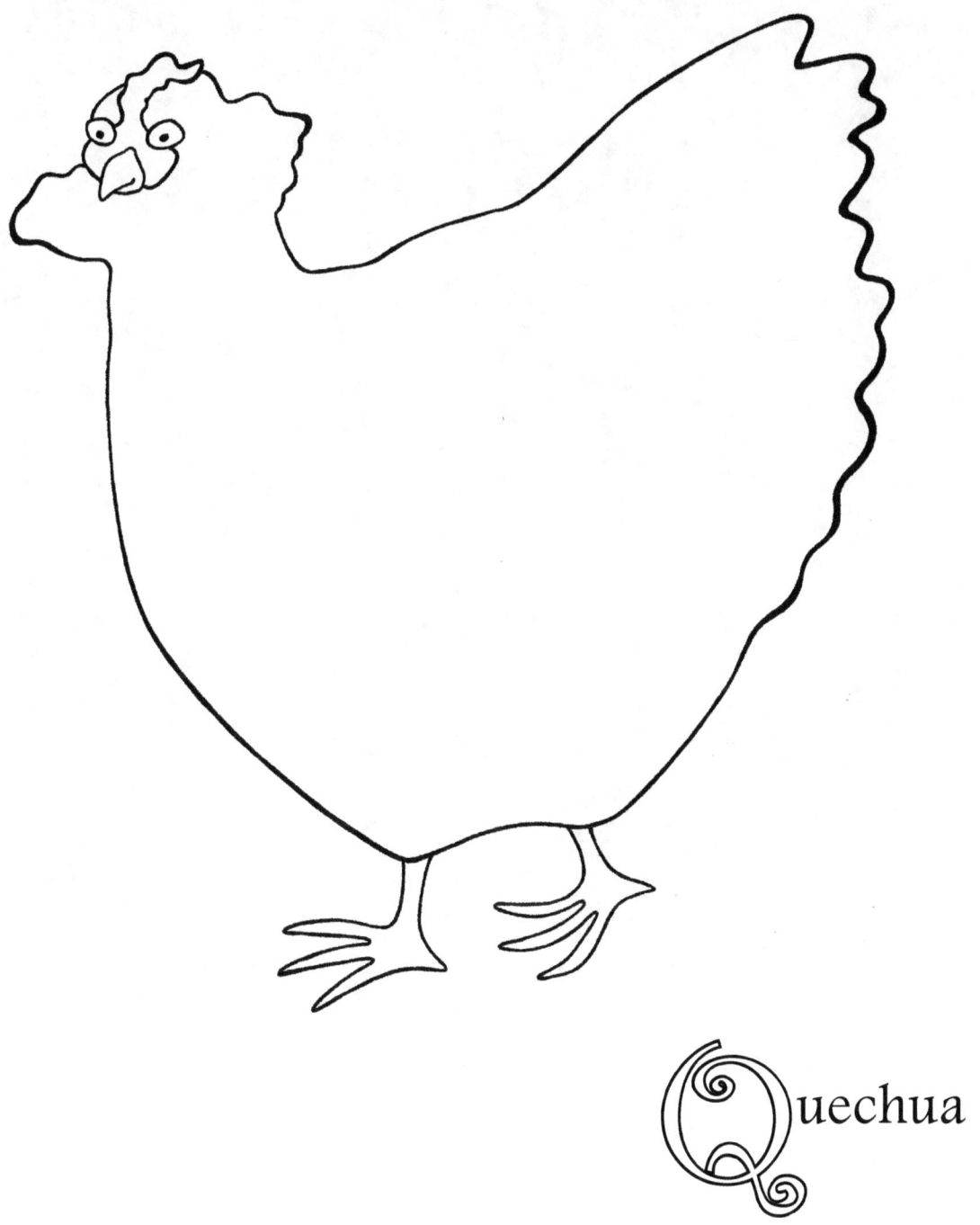

Quechua

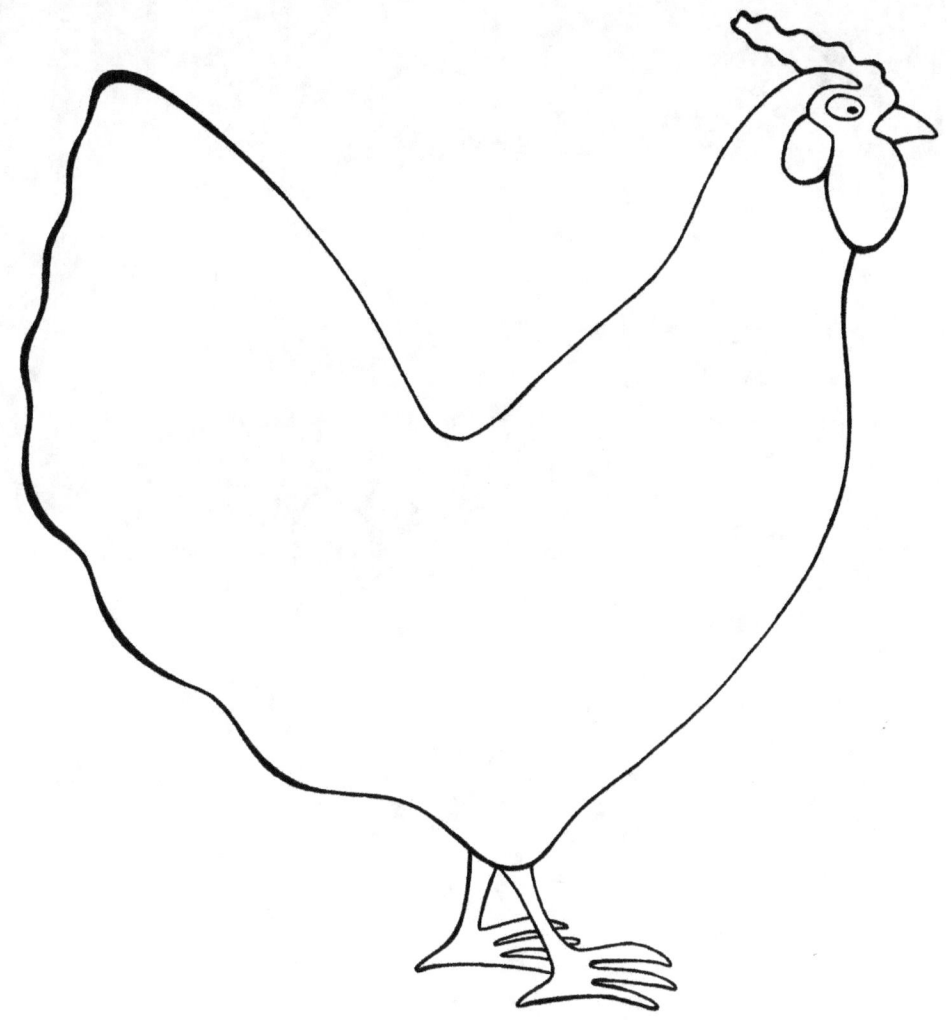

Rosecomb

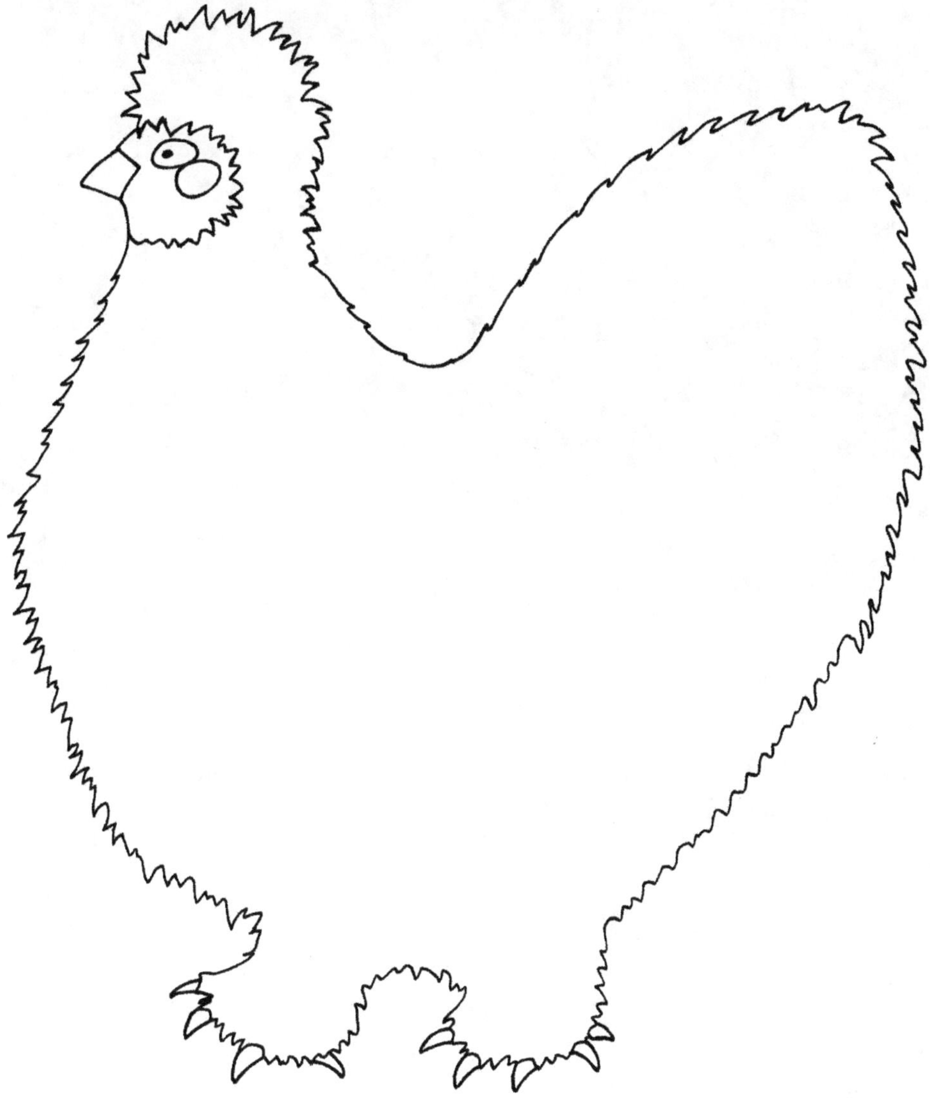

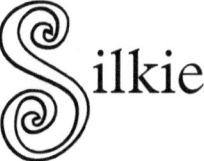

Silkie

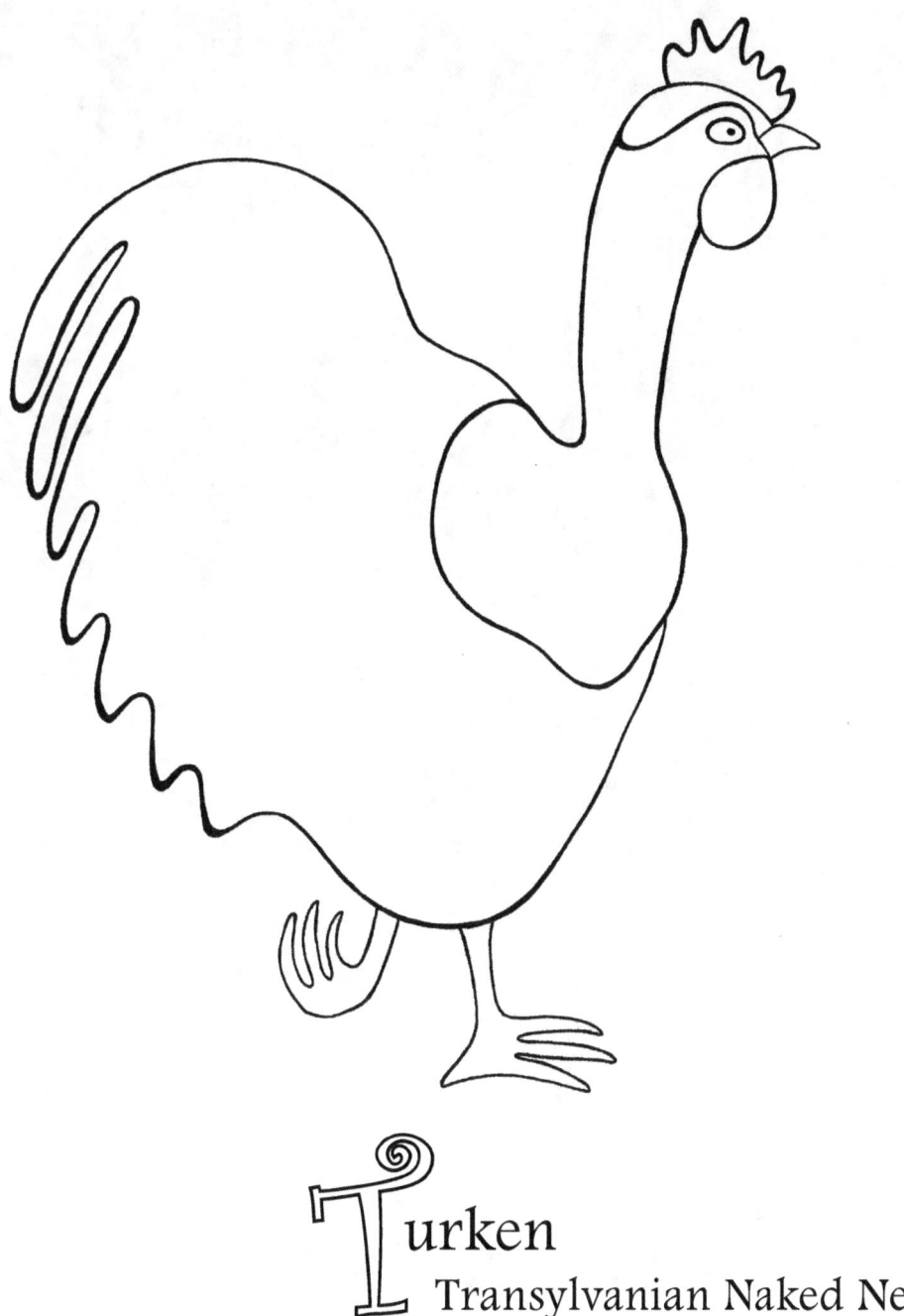

Turken
Transylvanian Naked Neck

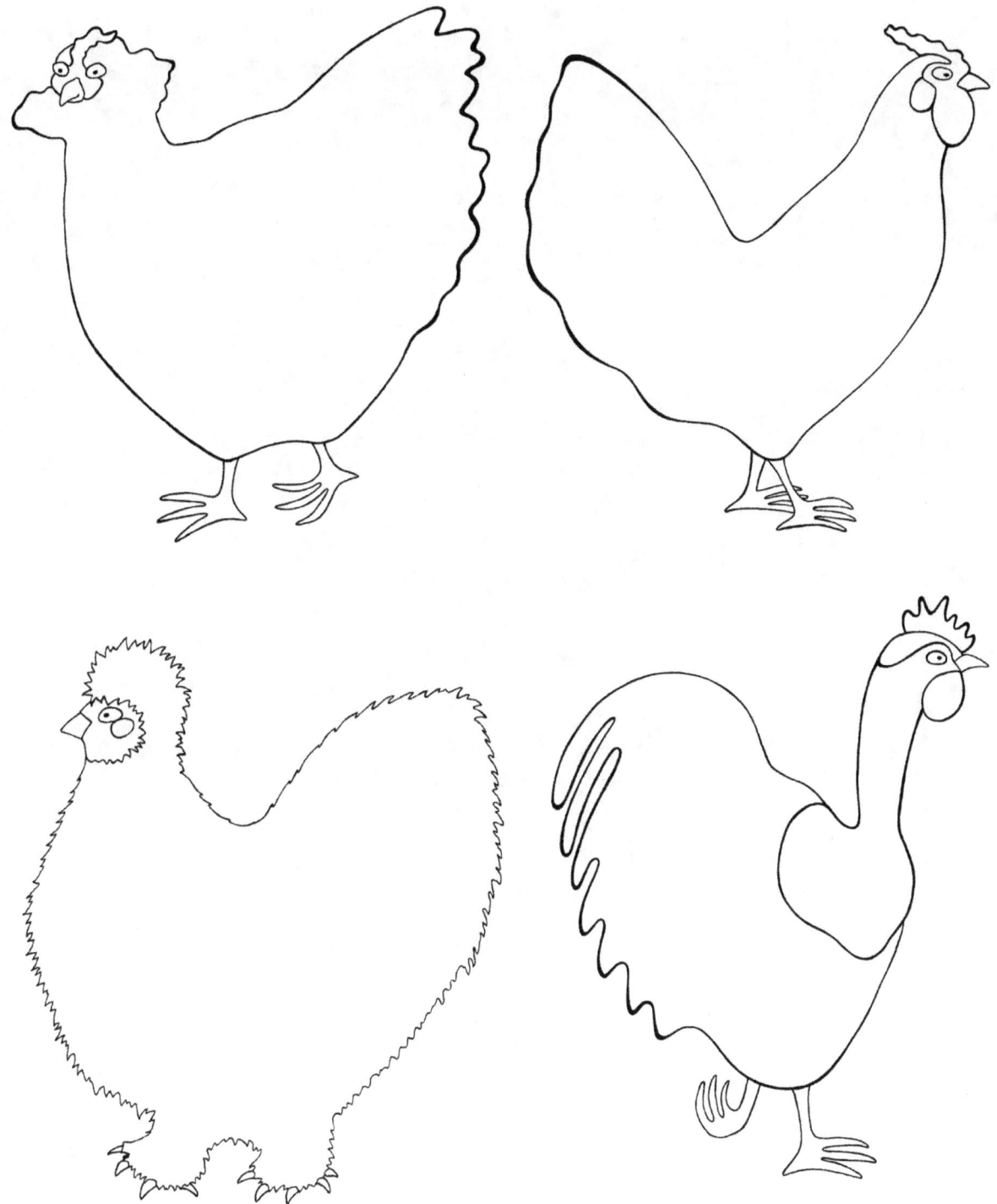

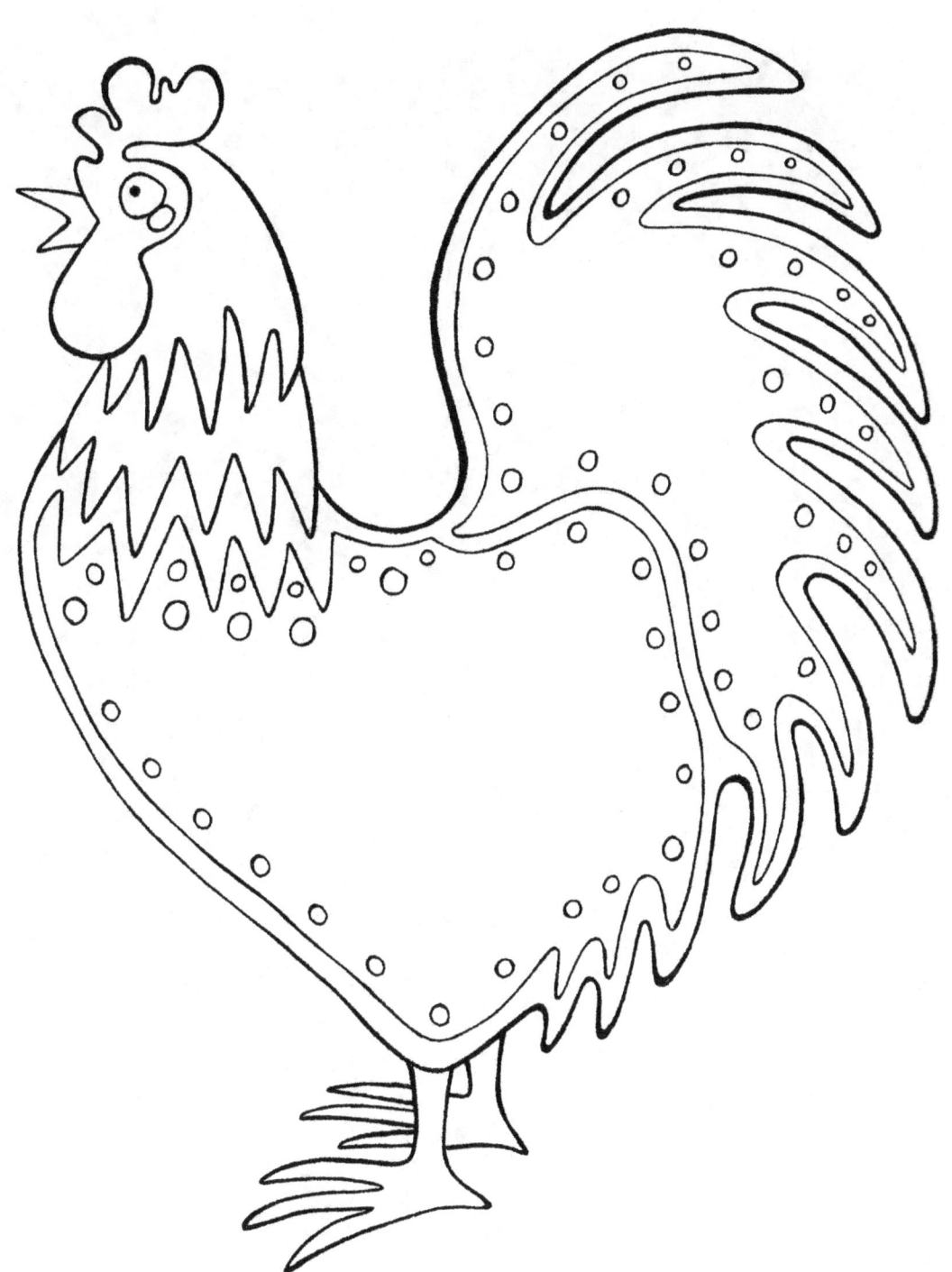

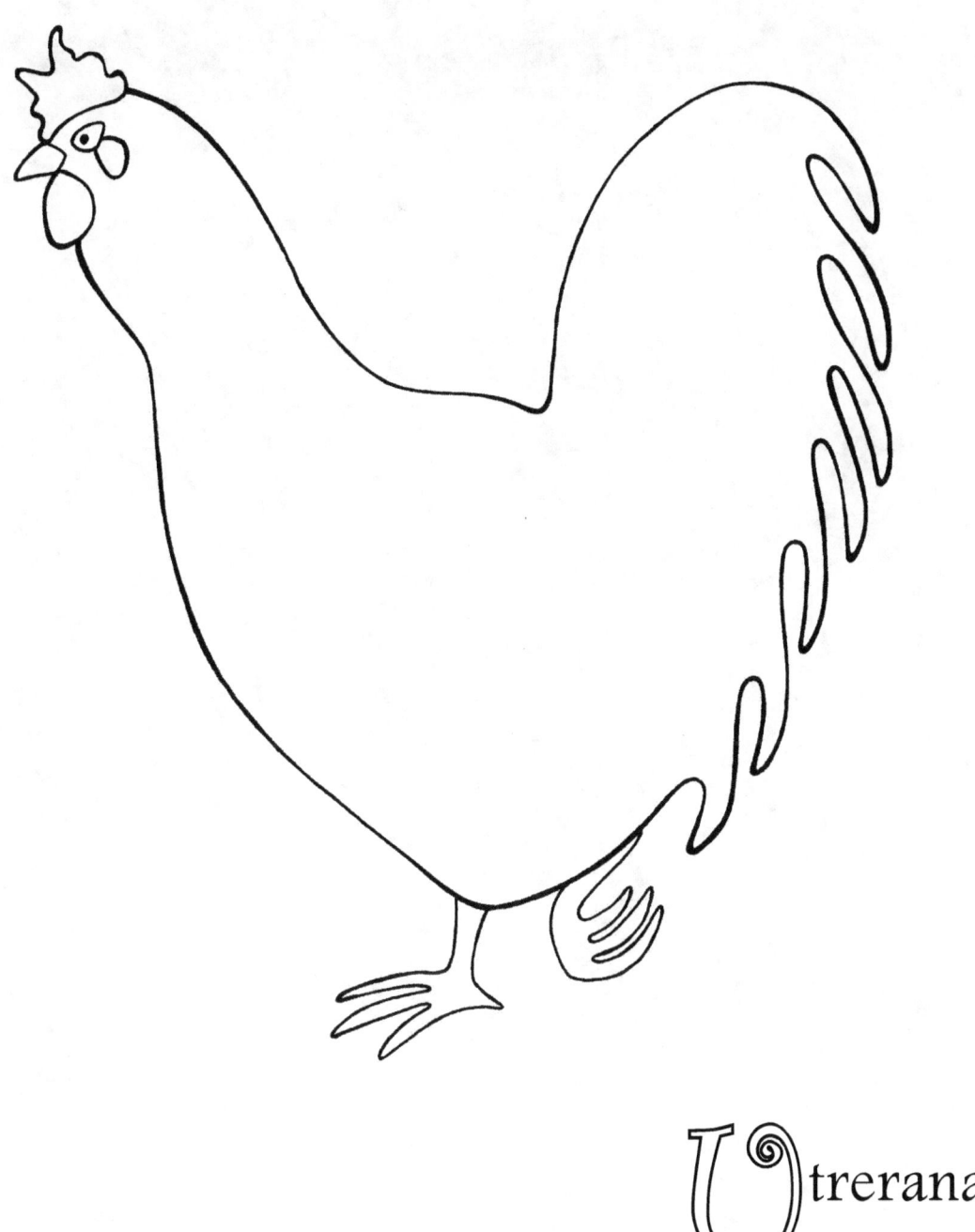

Utrerana

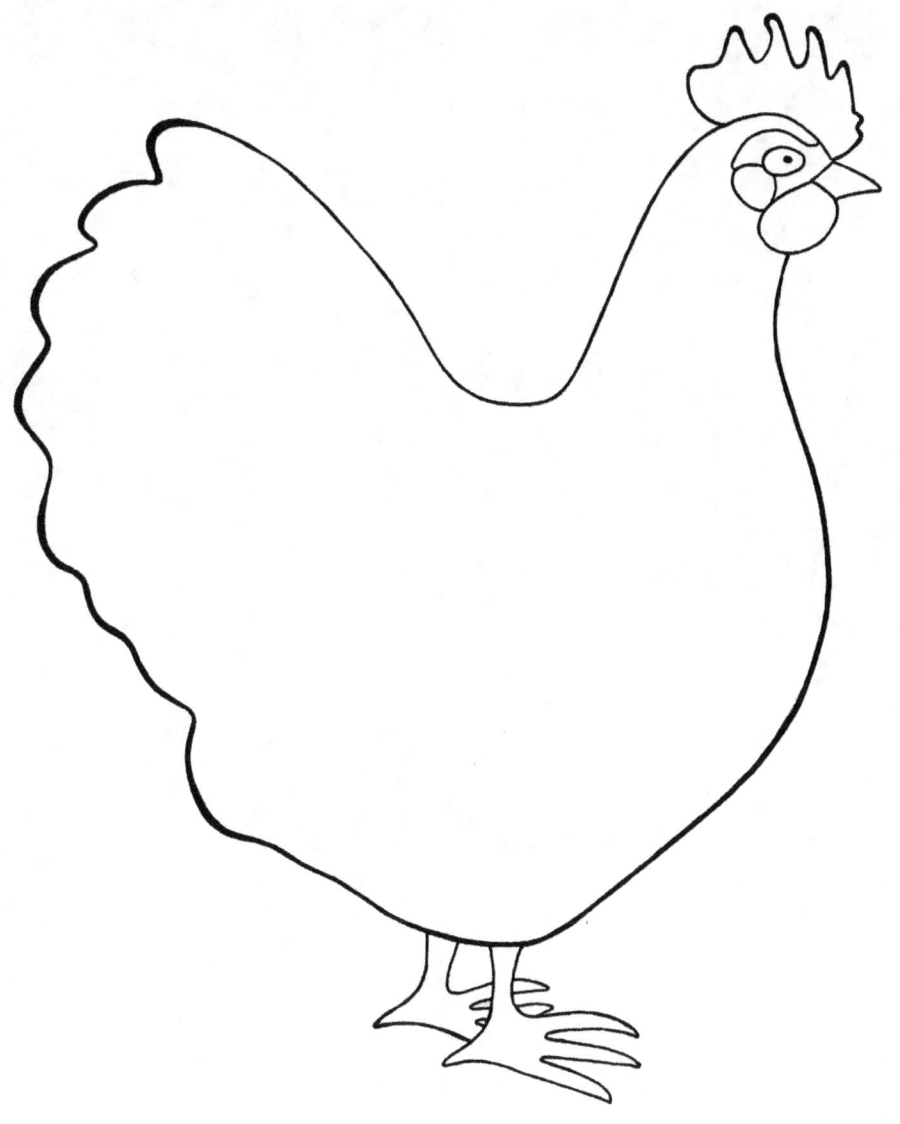

Vorwerk

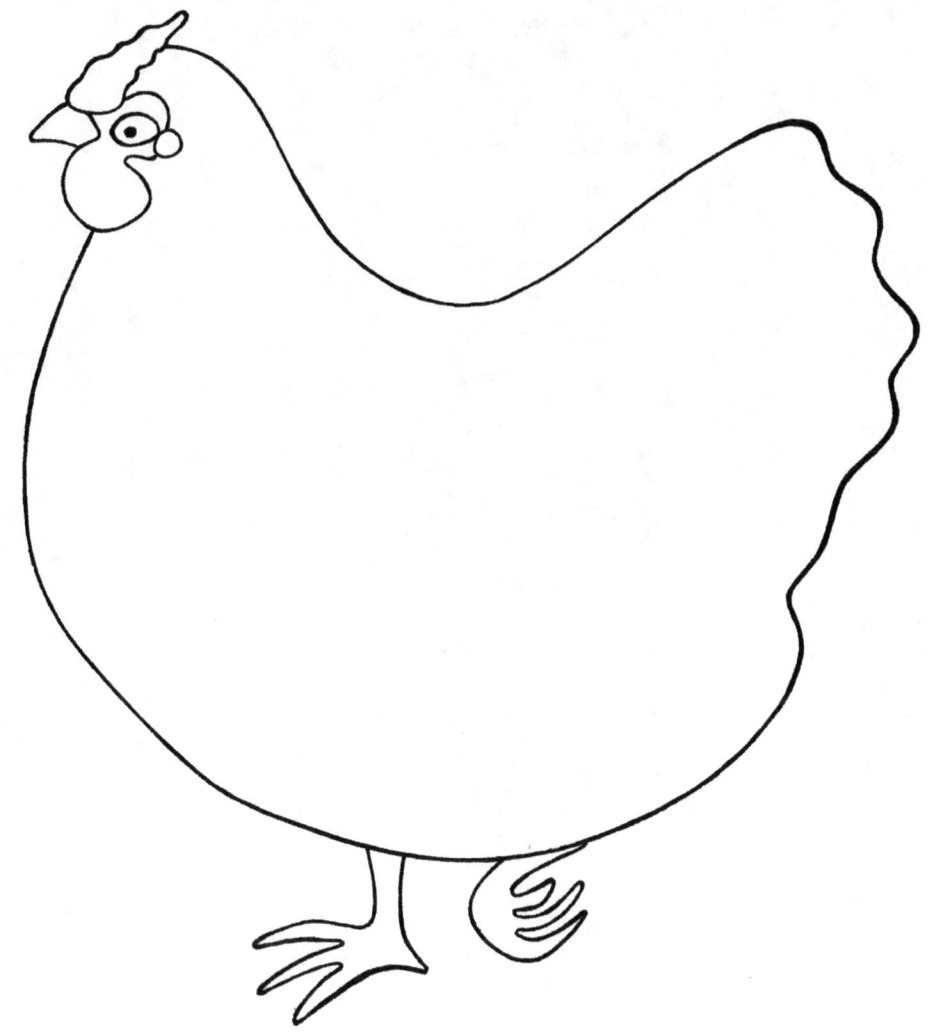

Wyandotte

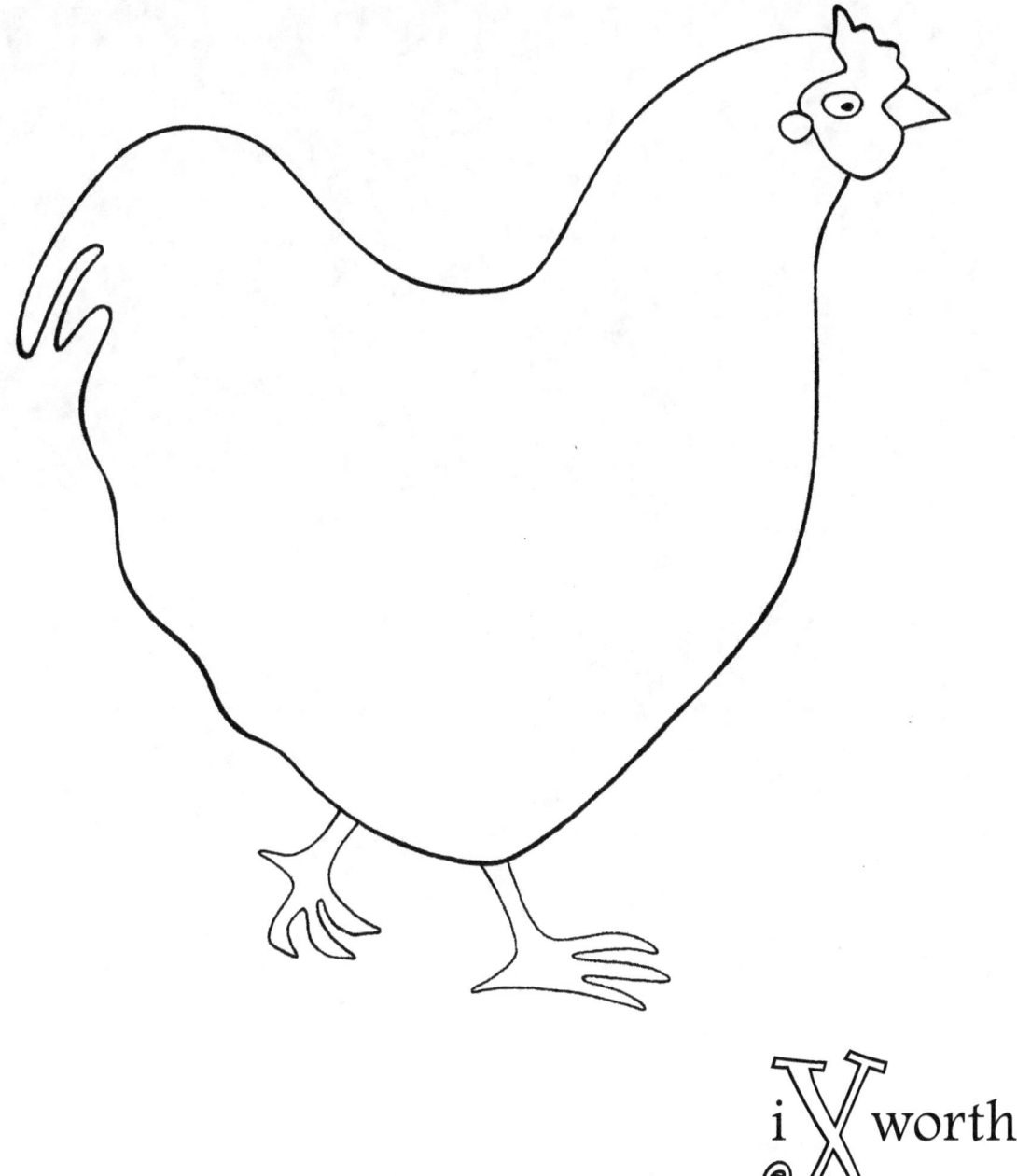

iXworth

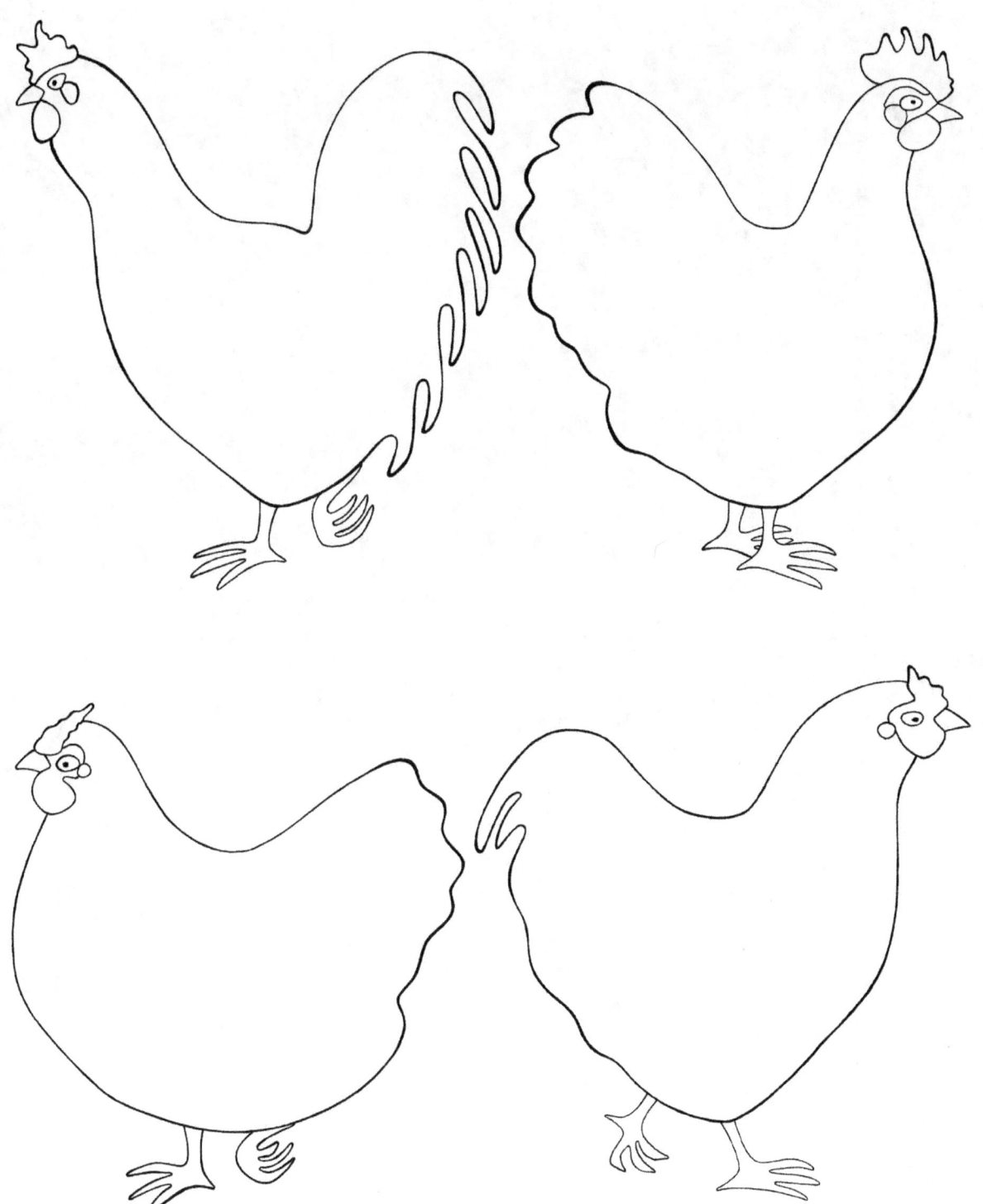

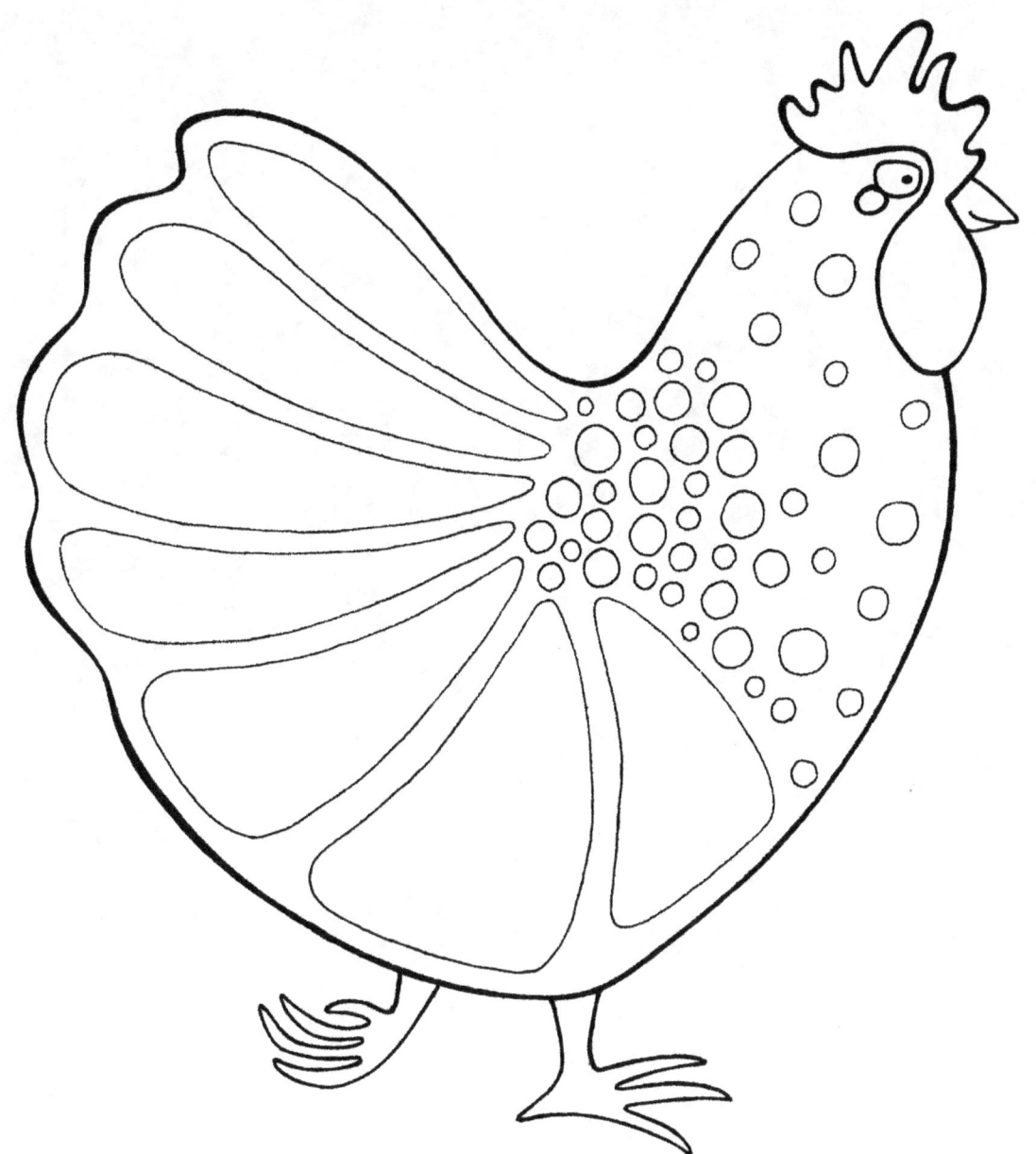

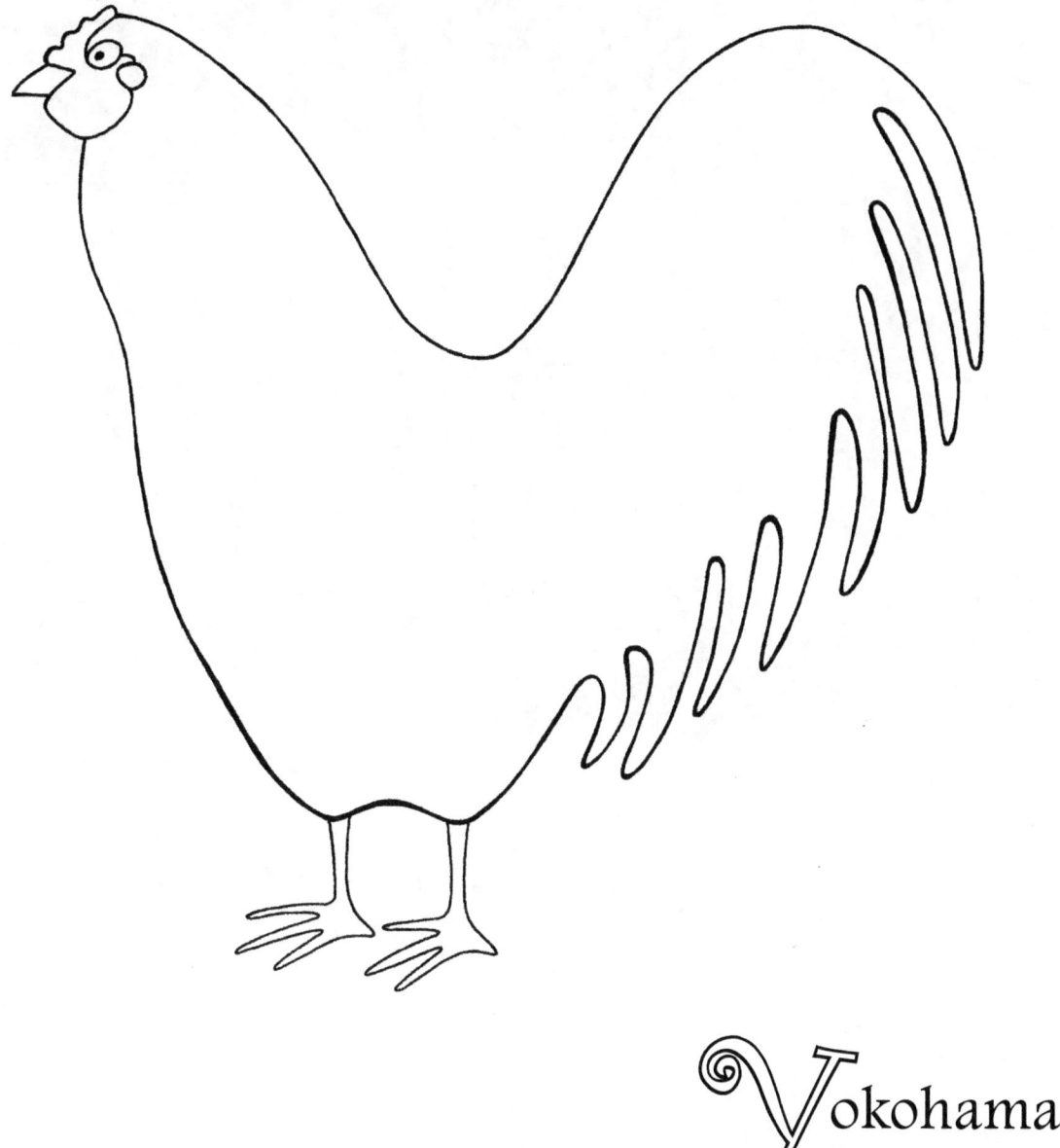

Yokohama

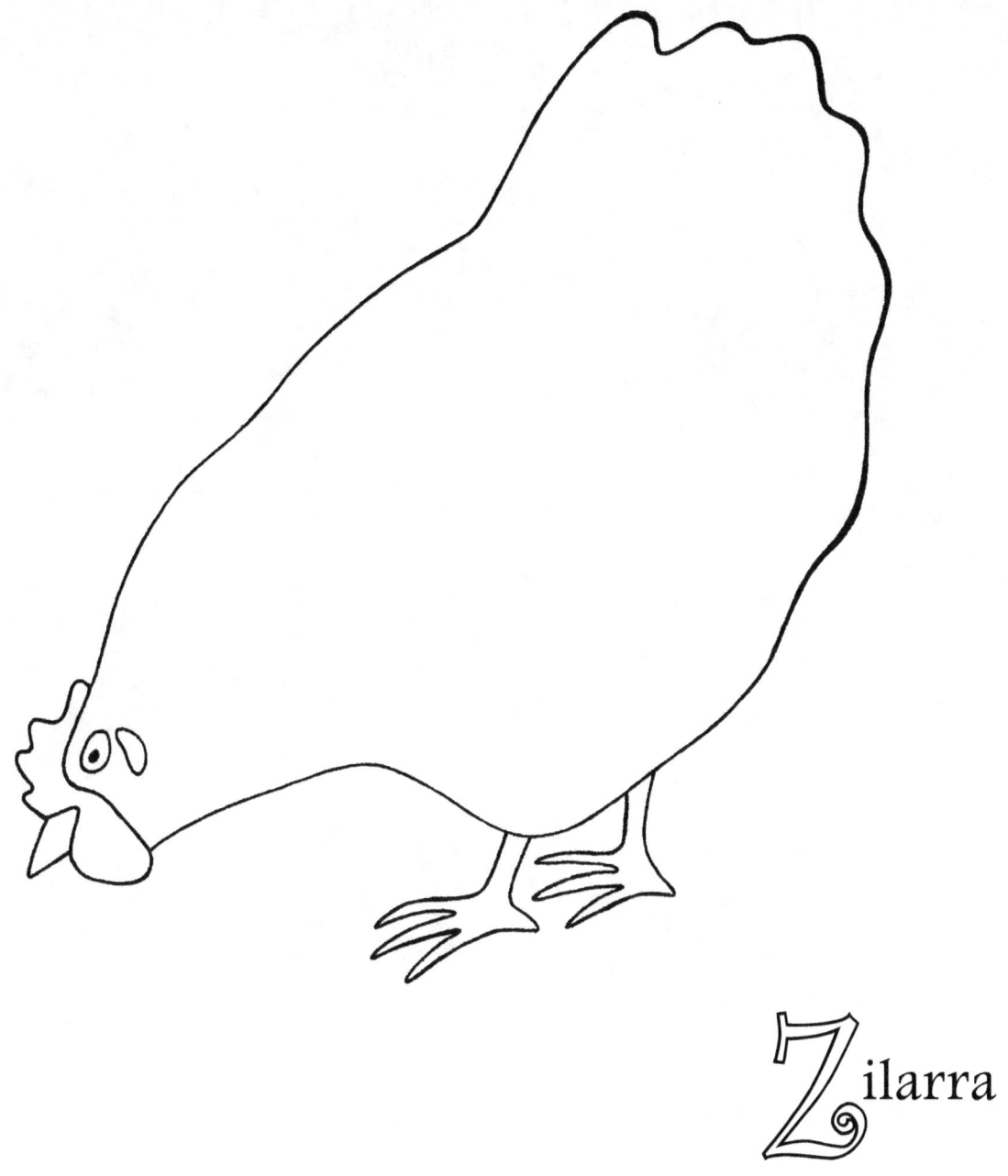

Zilarra

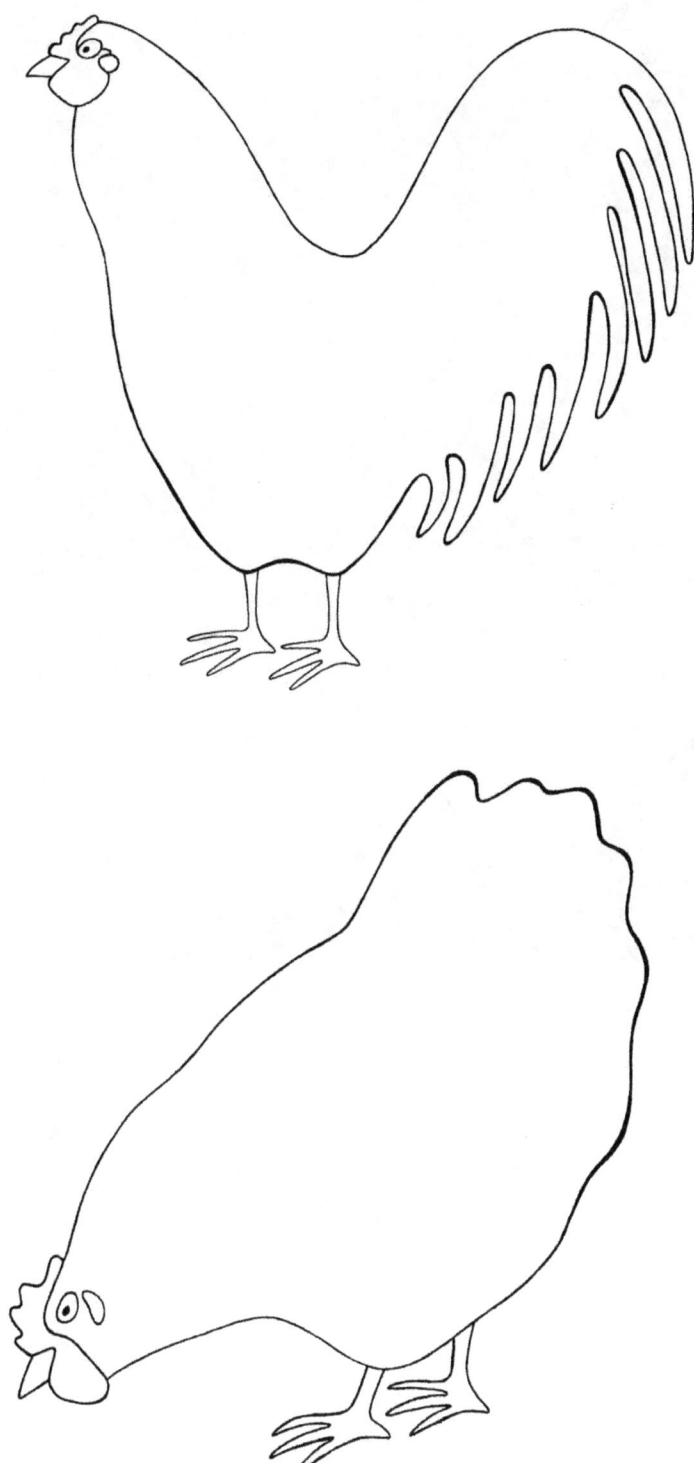

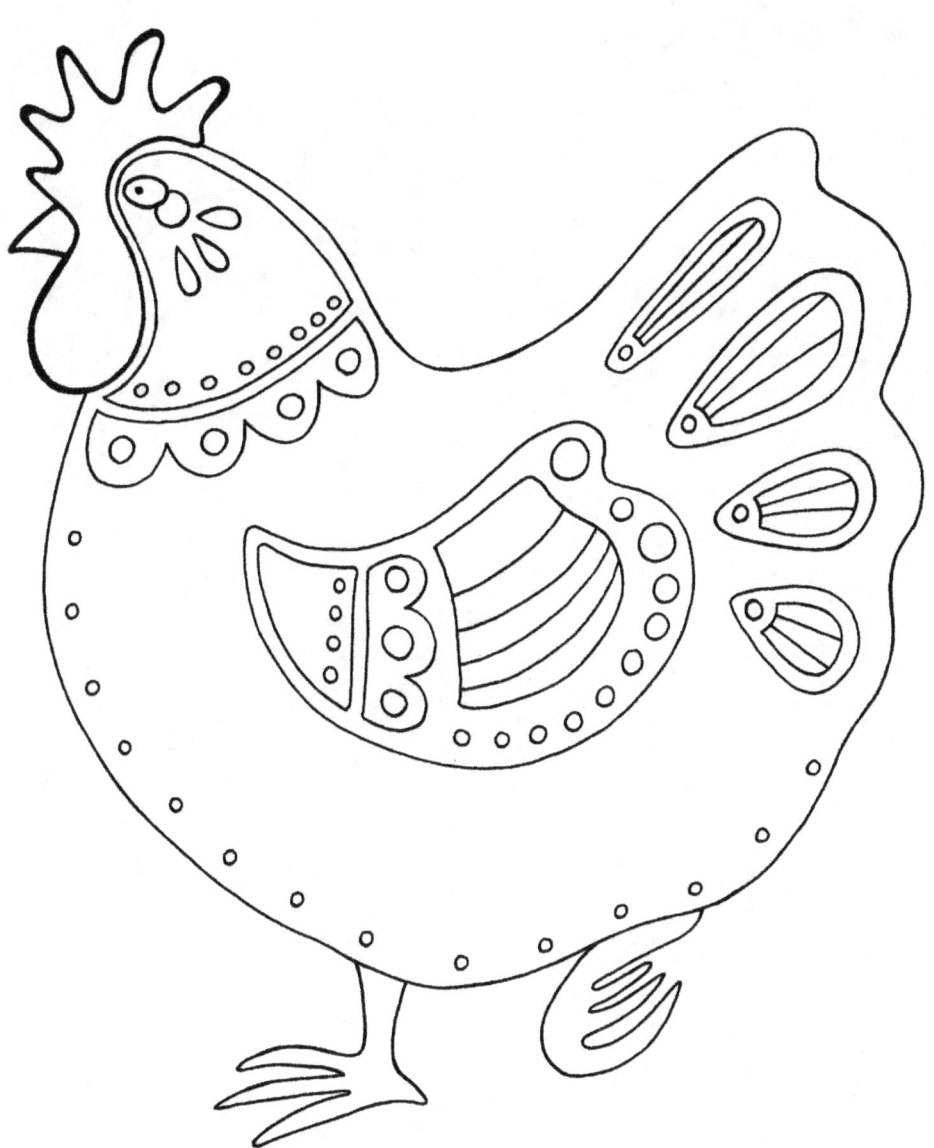

Friends and Foes

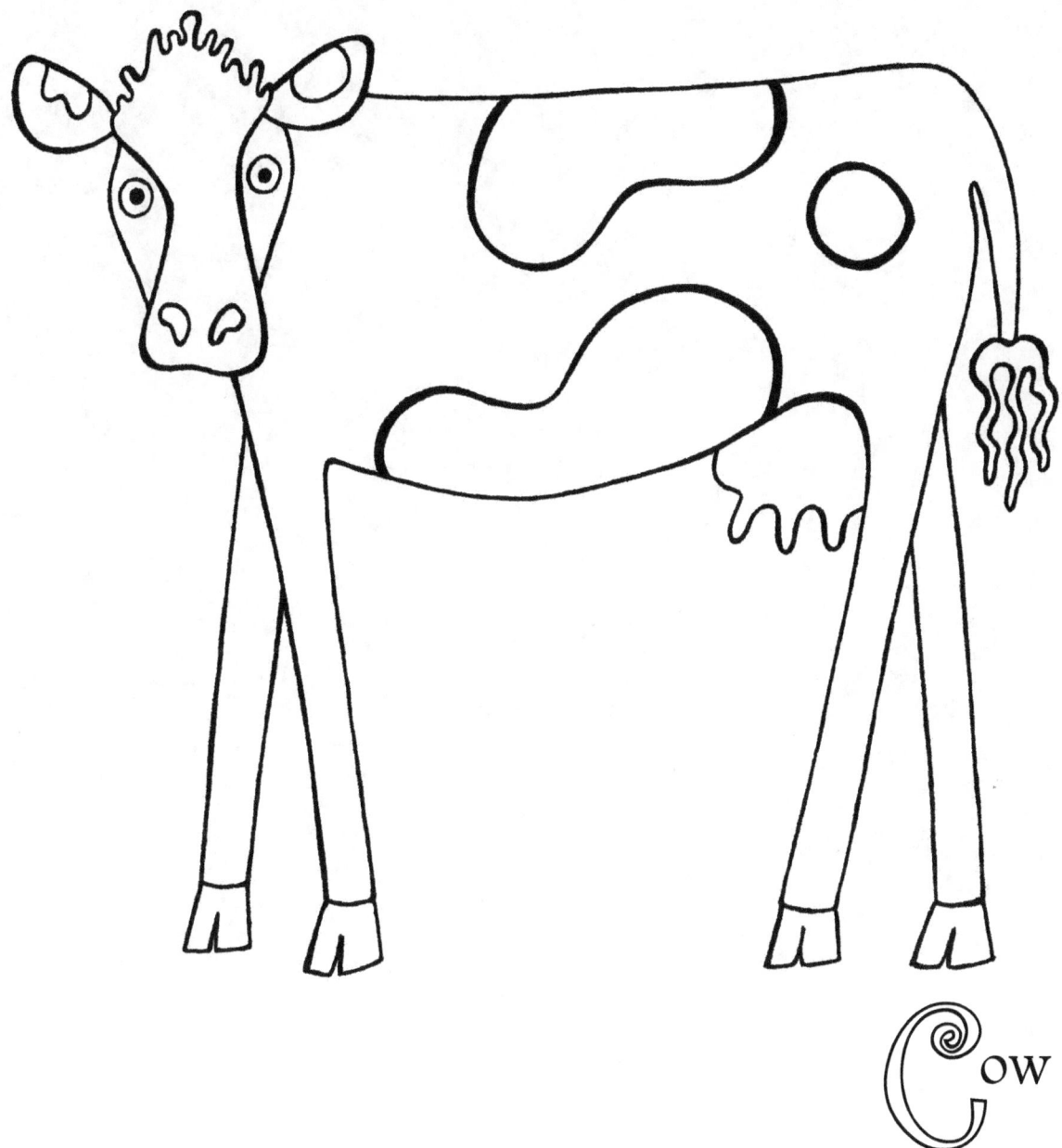

Cow

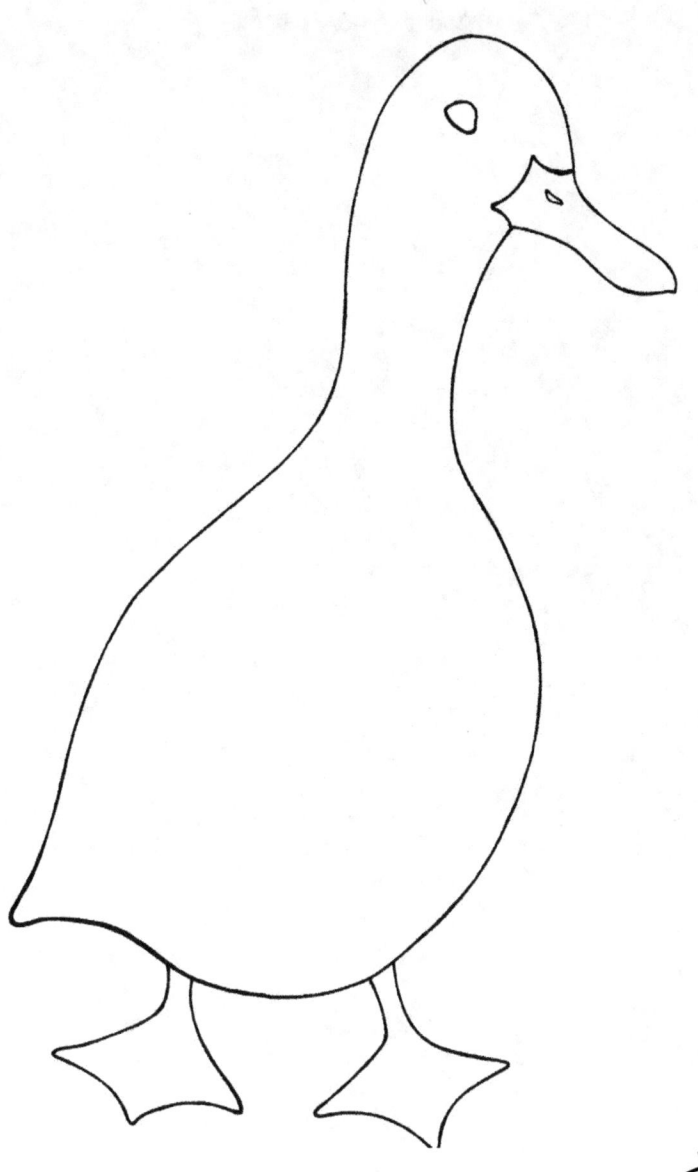

Duck

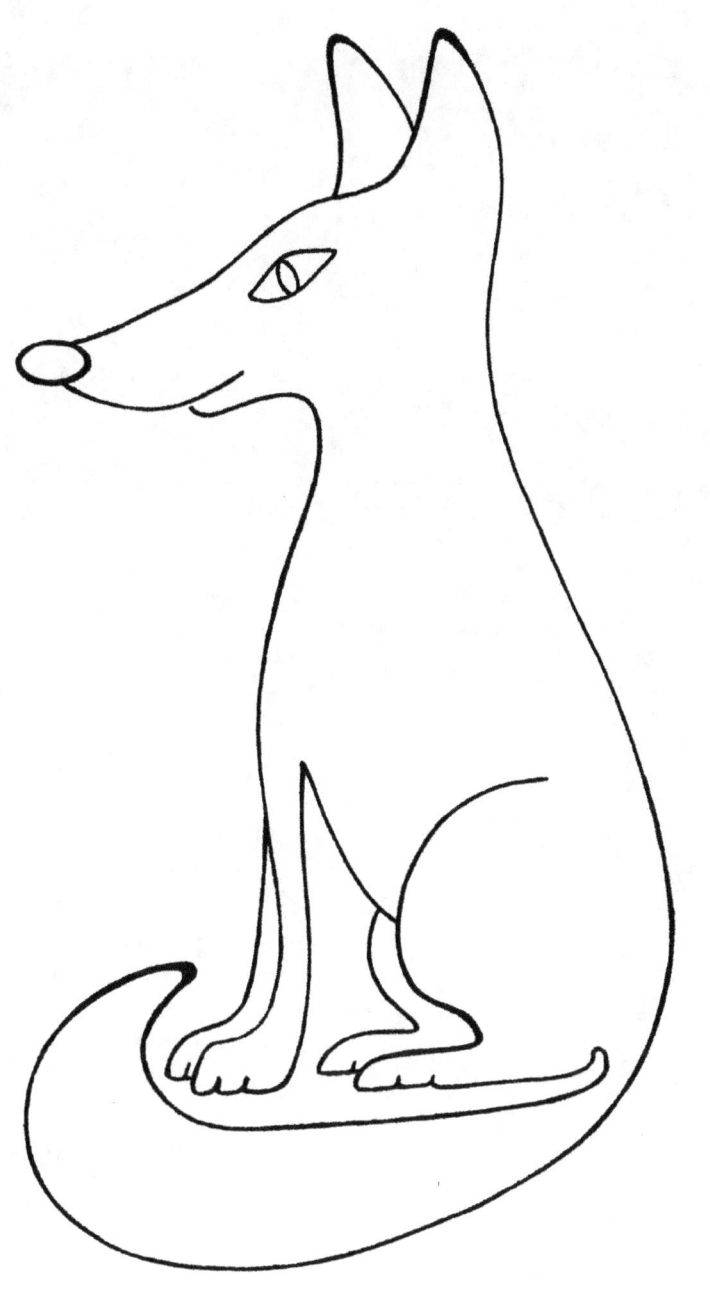

Fox

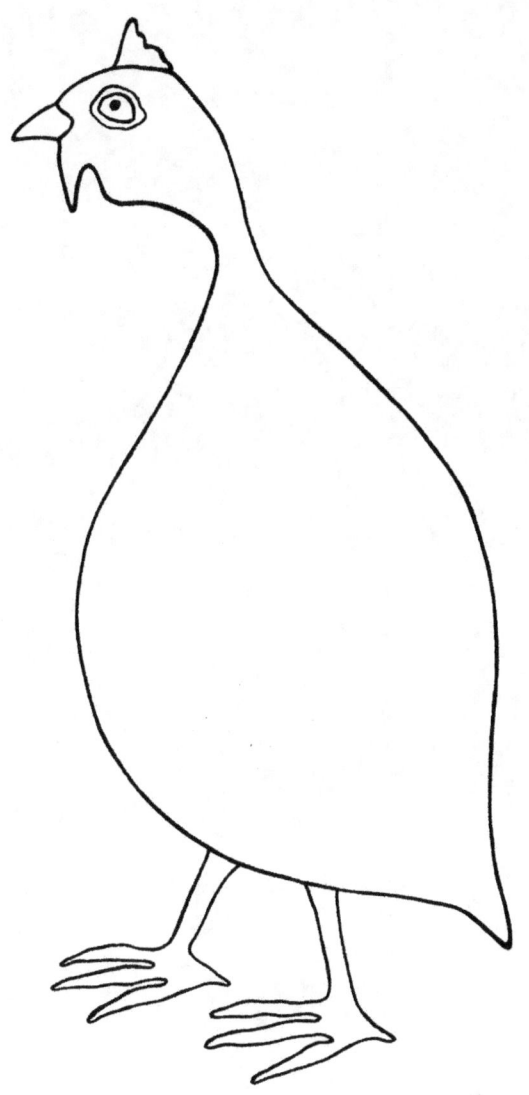

Guinea Hen

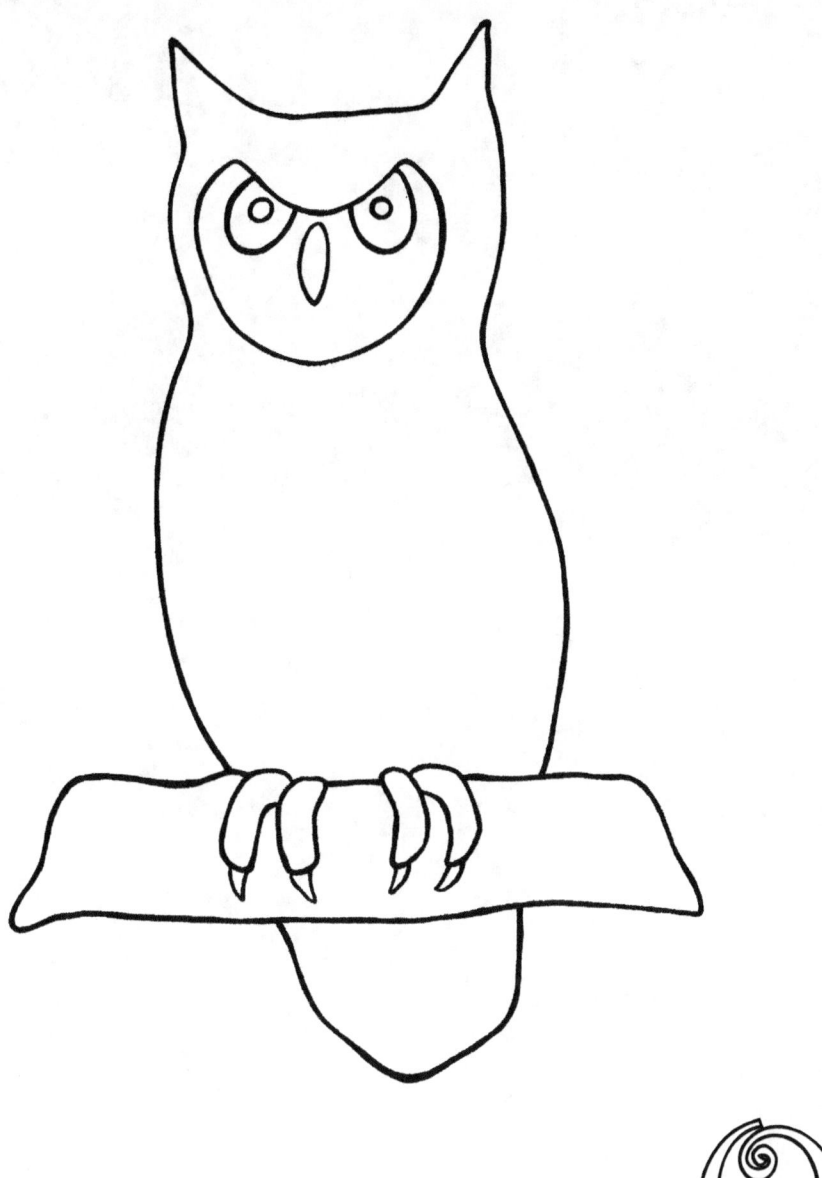

Owl

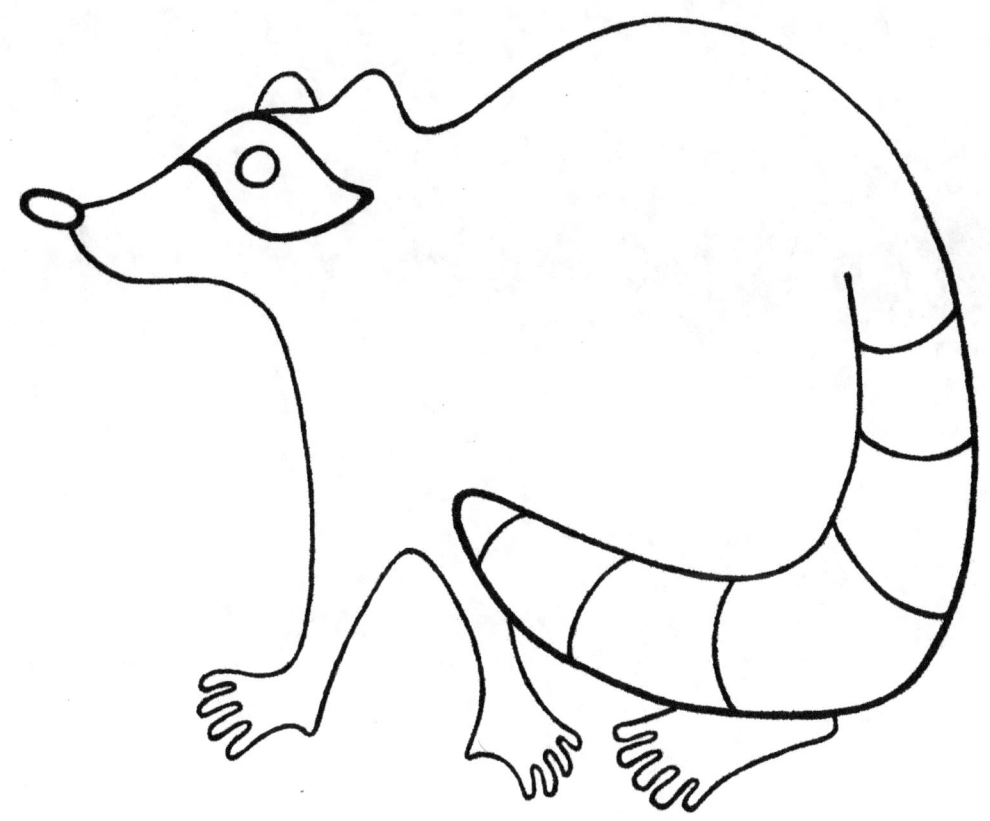

Raccoon

www.ingramcontent.com/pod-product-compliance
Lightning Source LLC
Chambersburg PA
CBHW080943170526
45158CB00008B/2362